AIR CAMPAIGN

CHROME DOME 1960–68

The B–52s' high-stakes Cold War nuclear operation

PETER E. DAVIES | ILLUSTRATED BY ADAM TOOBY

OSPREY PUBLISHING
Bloomsbury Publishing Plc
Kemp House, Chawley Park, Cumnor Hill, Oxford OX2 9PH, UK
29 Earlsfort Terrace, Dublin 2, Ireland
1385 Broadway, 5th Floor, New York, NY 10018, USA
E-mail: info@ospreypublishing.com
www.ospreypublishing.com

First published in Great Britain in 2024

A catalogue record for this book is available from the British Library.

ISBN: PB 9781472860545; eBook 9781472860552;
ePDF 9781472860569; XML 9781472860538

24 25 26 27 28 10 9 8 7 6 5 4 3 2 1

Maps by www.bounford.com
Diagrams by Adam Tooby
3D BEVs by Paul Kime
Index by Zoe Ross
Typeset by PDQ Digital Media Solutions, Bungay, UK
Printed and bound in India by Replika Press Private Ltd.

Title page: see caption on p.25.

CONTENTS

INTRODUCTION

The YB-52 with the original B-47-style tandem cockpit, which LeMay insisted on replacing with side-by-side seating in the B-52 for better crew coordination. Its wing structure was lighter than the Boeing B-47's but with a similar 35-degree sweepback. In B-52G/H versions, it contained a large fuel load, unlike the B-47's. A six-degree angle relative to the fuselage enabled non-rotation take-off with its unusual bicycle landing gear and outrigger wheels to support the 185ft wingspan. (USAF)

A KC-135 Airborne Command Post and nine Boeing B-47 Stratojet bombers lifted off from Offutt AFB and other Strategic Air Command (SAC) bases on February 3, 1961, leaving long, black smoke trails behind them. Eight hours later, they were replaced by other KC-135s and bombers in a routine that would keep SAC B-47s and their successors, Boeing B-52 Stratofortresses, on airborne alert until early 1968. SAC's ability to overfly the USSR with apparent impunity had been demonstrated by the 55th Reconnaissance Wing whose RB-47E/Hs had made 146 long-range flights from Thule, Greenland over the northern USSR from March to May 1956, gathering photographic and electronic intelligence. Their reconnaissance activities continued, but their primary role as bombers soon passed to the more capable B-52, hastened by structural failures in many B-47s.

In 1954, Secretary of the Air Force Donald Quarles described Boeing's B-52, which first flew on August 5 that year, as "the most formidable expression of air power in the history of military aviation." Almost 90 percent of the 742 B-52s built were delivered to the USAF by 1961. Seventy years later B-52s are still in the front line of the West's power projection, a role which they will retain for several more decades to come. As a primary weapon in at least four wars, not least the Cold War, the B-52 has acquired an unequalled reputation as both deterrent and ultimate "sledgehammer," armed with either nuclear or conventional weapons. Nuclear-armed bombers remain on ground alert, ready to hit pre-programmed targets in the event of a nuclear "first strike" on the United States in a war in which there could be no winners.

Strategic air power is used to influence the outcome of a conflict at long range, striking targets far behind the battle lines. Industrial facilities, power plants, seats of government, and their defenses become potential targets. Long-range bombers have been used since 1913 when Igor Sikorsky built the Ilya Mourometz bomber, which could carry over 1,000lb of bombs for 400 miles. The concept was slowly developed in the inter-war years. Many designers favored twin-engine bombers in the 1930s, but Boeing in Seattle,

This Boeing B-47E-85-BW (52-0469) entered SAC on July 22, 1954 and entered storage as an EB-47E after ten years' service. The B-47 was a challenging aircraft to fly and land. The crash on landing at RAF Lakenheath, UK of a 307th Bomb Wing *Reflex* B-47E (53-4230) on July 27, 1956 almost "turned part of Eastern England into a desert," according to a USAF general. The bomber crashed on a storage "igloo" containing three Mk 6 nuclear weapons, but the fire was extinguished before the bombs' 24,000lb of TNT could explode and spread radioactive material widely. (USAF)

Washington pioneered four-engine aircraft with greater range and increased payload. Boeing's B-17 and the Consolidated B-24 became primary weapons in the Allied bomber assault on Germany.

Among the bomb group commanders of the 8th Air Force's B-17 force in 1942 was Lt Col Curtis LeMay. Arriving shortly after the USAAF missions began, he was horrified at heavy Allied losses and inaccurate bombing. He believed that once war is declared a nation should hit the enemy hard and end the war quickly, arguing that the only realistic form of national defense was being able to strike a more decisive blow than any potential enemy could.

Boeing's much larger, technically advanced B-29 first flew in September 1942 and became the most expensive armament development program of World War II. Entering service in May 1944, it achieved 350mph and a range of 3,250 miles with bombloads approaching three times a B-17's. The Silverplate version of this Hemisphere Defense Weapon carried early nuclear weapons. When LeMay took over the 21st Air Force B-29 operation, he applied his hard-hitting doctrine, using his B-29 fleet to devastate Japanese cities with incendiary bombs. Acknowledging that some would call this 'uncivilized warfare,' LeMay avowed that his main priority was to protect his aircrews. He was under orders to "get results with the B-29," avoiding an invasion of Japan with the enormous losses it would entail. Initially, B-29s provided much-needed high-altitude reconnaissance over potential targets. Long-range reconnaissance remained a priority for all subsequent SAC heavy bombers.

Plans to use the 509th Composite Group's B-29s to drop an early atomic weapon were discussed with LeMay before the first one was tested in New Mexico in July 1945. As the only nuclear-capable group, the 509th CG took a major role in developing tactics for US atomic weapons. His fire-bombing campaign continued until the two *Little Boy* atom bombs were dropped, but he felt that it would have brought about Japanese surrender even without the nuclear weapons, since the Japanese were already attempting to use the USSR as an intermediary in peace talks. To underline the vital role of strategic bombing in securing a final surrender on August 14, a massive armada of 462 20th Air Force B-29s overflew the signing ceremony on USS *Misssouri*.

Postwar, LeMay still described himself as a "big bomber guy." He allegedly told his wife, who asked why he stayed with bombers, "Fighters are fun, but bombers are important." However, in his new role in the Pentagon within the RAND corporation, which generated new defense technology, he also encouraged the US intercontinental guided missile program, using the expertise of former Nazi scientists. In 1946, he accepted the concept of Mutually

Two prototypes of Convair's YB-60, essentially a swept-wing version of their piston-engine B-36 Peacemaker, were evaluated alongside the YB-52. It used the same J-57-P-3 engines. It first flew three days after the YB-52, but its performance was clearly inferior to the Stratofortress's, so it was canceled by October 2, 1952 when the XB-52 made its initial flight. (USAF)

Assured Destruction (MAD) which became a basic tenet of Cold War policy for both the USA and the Soviet Union. Ironically, the massive wartime air force, which gained independence from the US Army in July 1947, had been reduced to a fraction of its wartime peak of 2.4 million personnel. In 1946 it had only 17 nuclear-capable Silverplate B-29s and less than a dozen atom bombs.

LeMay's first major postwar task as commander of USAF Europe was organizing the Berlin Air Lift after the USSR closed the city off to the West. His concept of overwhelming opposition to aggression worked well, as Moscow finally backed down. Despite US President Truman's hopes that this would lead to an international ban on nuclear weapons, plans for US nuclear supremacy continued.

In 1948 LeMay took charge of SAC, which was suffering from inefficiency, absenteeism, a high accident rate, and inadequate training only two years after its creation. SAC had suffered considerably in 1947–48 due to funding cuts applied by Gen George C. Kenney. The force lost many non-flying officers, so their tasks had to be performed by pilots. Its officer complement was reduced to 5,100 officers in 1948, operating 420 bombers. LeMay strove to improve efficiency within SAC, introducing the command's Bombardment Competition in October 1949 to improve crews' performances. His rigid discipline involved frequent no-notice visits to SAC bases, where commanders would be instantly sacked if LeMay noticed the slightest deviation from the rules. Some crew members gained the impression that maintaining faultless personal appearance and immaculate uniforms was their main task.

LeMay improved morale through a "spot promotion" scheme for bomber crews. He introduced four crew categories, from "non-combat ready" up to "select," based on performance and bomb scores. Select crews were eligible for promotion, partly as a means of retaining expensively trained personnel for whom excellence became the norm. As another SAC leader, Gen Russell Dougherty, put it, "capability × will = deterrence."

Crews were only achieving acceptable practice bombing results by flying against established dummy targets at around 15,000ft, altitudes which would have been lethal for them over defended territory. LeMay realized that, in the event of war, the available B-29s would have to fly to the US civilian Atomic Energy Commission's weapons store at Fort Hood, Texas or, later, to the Manzano nuclear storage facility at Kirtland AFB, New Mexico to be loaded with atomic bombs. They would have then flown to Newfoundland or the UK to embark upon their missions. From 1956, custody of the weapons was instead entrusted to SAC.

For B-29 crews, these would have been one-way missions, as their planes lacked the range to return to their bases. There was no provision for a nuclear alert force to deal with a surprise attack by Soviet bombers. Loading a five-ton Mk 3 *Fat Man* nuclear weapon into a B-29 or B-50 was almost a one-hour task. Each bomb took a large team two days to assemble and it had to be disassembled after nine days, as its batteries began to corrode.

To demonstrate the severity of the problem, LeMay arranged the "Dayton Exercise." The entire SAC fleet was ordered to conduct a simulated, high-altitude radar-bombing strike on Wright Field at Dayton, Ohio. Many of the B-29s were either unserviceable or aborted with mechanical problems. Some reached the target, but out of 303 bombing runs not a single bomber scored a hit and two-thirds were more than 7,000ft off target. The average bombing error was 1.9 miles. Curtis LeMay resolved to galvanize SAC's performance, stating, "We are at war now!" He replaced many senior officers with strict disciplinarians like Gen Thomas S. Power, who was LeMay's deputy and became his successor. Power was even more extreme in insisting upon SAC's pre-eminence in gaining budgetary priorities and tended to rule by fear. Two years later, a similar but tightly organized exercise involving all SAC's resources achieved better results. In one of Power's salutary comments on the Cold War, he stated, "At the end of the war if there are two Americans and one Russian left alive, we win!"

In LeMay's new regime, rules were tightened to the point where failure, including his own, was unacceptable and individual crew initiative was suppressed. However, he improved living conditions for his airmen by supplementing Congressional funding with fund-raising

B-52D-075-BO 56-0608 being prepared for an early take-off from Glasgow AFB, Montana with the 91st BW. Transferred to the 99th BW at Westover AFB it became a *Linebacker II* casualty detached to the 307th BW on December 19, 1972 while attacking the Hanoi radio station. An SA-2 hit it during its post-target turn, with its protective counter-measures radiation directed away from the threat. Two crew members were killed and four became prisoners. (USAF)

activities such as public Sports Car of America races at SAC bases. To one of his many critics LeMay became the "caveman in the jet bomber," but over the following decade he built SAC into a huge, tightly regulated war machine equipped with the most advanced weapons available, including four generations of strategic bombers. Each one was a major advance on its predecessor, and all were forcefully promoted by LeMay in the fight for the colossal Congressional funding required to develop radically new technologies quickly. Other USAF commands, notably Tactical Air Command, were less favored in funding debates.

The Korean War, which LeMay regarded as the sort of small-scale conflict in which SAC should not be involved, showed how quickly the B-29 had dated. However, it was the only long-range bomber available to attack targets in North Korea. LeMay was ordered to send two SAC units, which were withdrawn after losses to communist MiG-15 jets.

The first B-29 (an uprated B-50) replacement was the piston-engine Convair B-36, a 230ft-wingspan giant with an 86,000lb bombload and the endurance to conduct regular missions lasting up to 32 hours without refueling. It was funded by Congress in highly controversial circumstances, which followed the Navy's loss of its projected USS *United States* aircraft carrier, its intended platform for its nuclear air force. By using forward bases such as Guam, all Soviet cities were within range of bomber and reconnaissance B-36s, but they were relatively slow and the advent of improved Soviet jet fighters during the 1950s made the Convair leviathan too vulnerable.

Airborne alert

LeMay repeated his simulated Emergency War Orders nuclear attack exercises against American cities with considerable success and demonstrated the B-36's range in several record-breaking flights. Airborne alert missions, which evolved into *Chrome Dome*, began when B-36s of the 72nd BW(H) flew from their Ramey, Puerto Rico base to Nouasseur, Morocco and back. Intercontinental range was the deciding factor for LeMay who, in defending the B-36 at a Congressional hearing where many wished to cancel it, stated that he preferred it to its successor, the jet-powered but shorter-ranged Boeing B-47 medium bomber.

Although Boeing began work on its Model 413 (effectively a jet-powered B-29) in 1943, captured German data on swept-wing flight enabled it to submit the Model 448 on September 6, 1945, featuring swept flying surfaces and various jet engine configurations. These studies led to two prototype XB-47s, requested by the USAAF Engineering Division. With six J35 jet engines, swept wings, and tail surfaces, the aircraft first flew on December 17, 1947. Although its 600mph top speed was a significant advance on the B-36, its unrefueled range of 4,000 miles with 10,000lb of ordnance fell short of LeMay's need for an intercontinental bomber.

Nevertheless, over 2,000 were ordered to swell SAC's burgeoning power and to take it into the jet age. By 1956, more than 1,500 B/RB-47s had been equipped with SAC units. The B-47 bomber and specialized SAC RB-47 reconnaissance versions lasted until December 1967, by which time their B/RB-52 successors, the primary weapons of Cold War nuclear defense, were fully established in service and able to initiate the *Chrome Dome* airborne alert mission.

Stratofortress

The Boeing B-52, which reflected the very fast pace of military technology in the 1940s, originated in World War II when it was assumed that Nazi victory in Europe and the UK would mean that retaliatory bombing missions would have to be launched from US bases. Although the major American aircraft companies were preoccupied with manufacturing established bomber types until 1945, some development work continued. The "interim" B-36, B-47, and Northrop's rejected XB-35 Flying Wing resulted from that.

US Cold War bomber strength is represented here by a B-47A (left), a B-58A Hustler (top) and a B-52 – in this case NASA's famous NB-52B 52-0008 "Balls 8," used for many launches of experimental aircraft. The formation is completed by a Tactical Air Command Douglas B-66, a medium-range nuclear attacker. (USAF)

Boeing experimented with numerous combinations of jet and turboprop propulsion and different wing types. The B-47's swept wing type was generally accepted as ideal for optimum speed and low drag, but LeMay, Air Materiel Command, and the USAAF's Chief of Bomber Development Col Henry Warden demanded a larger aircraft was developed. In October 1948 Col Warden encouraged Pratt &Whitney to develop a new 10,000lb thrust turbojet, the J57, to replace the turboprops that Boeing designers had planned for their Model 464 in response to the USAAF's February 13, 1946 request for proposals for a longer-ranging bomber. On October 21 Boeing's chief designers, George Schairer and Ed Wells, met Warden and heard of the proposed switch to turbojet propulsion. In a brain-storming weekend session at the Van Cleve Hotel, Seattle, the six-man Boeing design team came up with the Model 464-49. Their balsa wood model miniaturized a bomber with eight pod-mounted J57-P-3 engines and a thicker, swept wing of 4,000 sq ft, almost three times the area of the B-47's thin wing. The Model 464-49-0 was intended to weigh 330,000lb, carry 10,000lb of bombs over 8,000 miles unrefueled and reach 572mph with a service ceiling of around 45,000ft. Warden secured approval and an order for a full-scale XB-52 Stratofortress mock-up. Le May, seeing it as his ideal bomber, recommended it to the Air Force in 1950 and suppressed further B-47 development. The immediate success of the prototype YB-52 after its first flight on April 15, 1952 meant that Convair's back-up YB-60 program could be canceled.

SAC planning also proceeded in another direction during the early 1950s. The Wright Air Development Center predicted that rapid development of Soviet ground-to-air missiles such as the SA-2 Guideline and its successors would render all strategic bombers obsolete by 1960. LeMay's response was to demand a Mach 3 supersonic bomber force that would fly above the missiles, outpacing their radar tracking systems. Boeing's MX-1022 study in 1950 proposed a large bomber, capable of a supersonic dash to a target at high altitude, outdistancing interceptors and defeating antiaircraft tracking radars.

Convair's rival MX-1964 proposal did lead to a supersonic bomber, the delta-winged B-58 Hustler with four podded, afterburning J79 engines and Mach 2 speed at 40,000ft. At low

Gen Curtis LeMay (center) and Gen Thomas Power meet President John F. Kennedy at SAC HQ. The success of LeMay's aerial campaign against Japan proved the supremacy of the bomber as a decisive weapon and strongly influenced the creation of the US Air Force as a separate organization from the Army, with Strategic Air Command as its primary element. (USAF)

altitude, avoiding the increasingly sophisticated Soviet radars, it could attain 600mph, but with severely reduced endurance. Several tankers were needed for it to reach the nearest Soviet targets via the Arctic routes. An accident rate that wiped out a quarter of the 116 B-58As, together with spiralling maintenance costs three times greater than the B-52's, limited its active service to only eight years.

In March 1956, at a time when the USAF was receiving 46 percent of the US defense budget, Air Force chiefs debated funding for a developed B-52, the B-52G with a 30 percent range increase and greatly improved maintenance man-hours. This was seen as a comparatively short-term solution to SAC's needs, as was the purchase of 76 swing-wing FB-111As in 1965 to replace the B-58As and remaining B-47s.

The long-term objective was to replace the B-52 altogether with a completely new long-range bomber. Early Stratofortress versions up to the B-52F were stored by 1970. Opposition to a replacement came from proponents of the Titan and Atlas intercontinental ballistic missiles (ICBMs) and the US Navy, which wanted to give its new Polaris missile submarines nuclear capability. Whereas the USAF had controversially won 67 percent of the defense budget between 1954 and 1958, the USN received a larger share in 1958–59, reducing SAC's funding.

LeMay continued to press for a new Mach 3 strategic bomber. Various highly advanced solutions, including nuclear-heated air for enhanced thrust and boron-based fuels, were explored for suitable powerplants. In March 1956 Boeing proposed revolutionary designs including the Model 724-13, an extraordinary 200ft-long aircraft with disposable 55ft outer wing sections containing fuel and supporting 76ft-long drop tanks.

North American Aviation produced the delta-winged XB-70, with six 28,000lb thrust YJ93 turbojets, in January 1958. An in-service date of 1965 was projected, two years after LeMay's deadline. Its designers faced enormous technical challenges, soaring costs, and growing criticism in their efforts to achieve Mach 3 dash speed performance at 80,000ft over a 6,873-mile range. Testing in 1966 included a sustained Mach 3 dash lasting 32 minutes, reaching 74,000ft. Dwindling support within the Eisenhower administration was combined with doubts that speed alone would defeat Soviet missile defenses. The XB-70's spiralling costs combined with an increasingly massive budget for ICBMs brought the program close to cancelation in 1959. LeMay's influence in Congress had been reduced by disputes over USAF pay, and he lacked allies to defend the "big bomber" program. He left his post in July 1957, before SAC's Atlas ICBMs were activated within SAC.

However, Gen Thomas White, USAF Chief of Staff in 1960, promoted the flexibility of the bomber compared with a one-shot ICBM that could not be recalled in an emergency. Bomber crews, he argued, under SAC's "Positive Control" procedure, could only take off on nuclear missions under presidential orders and only proceed to their targets on receipt of the "go code" from the highest authority. Without that authority they would return to base.

Gen White and Lt Gen Wilson (Deputy Chief of Staff, Development) persuaded Congress of the advisability of a mixed force of ICBMs, B-52s, and B-70s, but President John F. Kennedy's appointment of Robert McNamara as Secretary of Defense, on condition that McNamara would have complete control of defense procurement, altered SAC's plans radically. The XB-70 was reduced to a research program. Doubts about high-altitude bombers increased markedly following the shooting down of Gary Powers' U-2 spy-plane by a Soviet SA-2 missile and the knowledge that the USSR was developing a high-altitude Mach 3 interceptor, the MiG-25. McNamara, intent on promoting cost-saving ICBMs rather than bombers, but also far more cautious about the possibility of using nuclear weapons than many of his contemporaries, advocated the cheaper carriage of the unproven, stand-off Skybolt missile by low-flying B-52s instead of the XB-70, which was duly canceled in March 1961. Throughout the missile vs bomber debates, LeMay and other SAC commanders pointed out that ICBMs, unlike bombers, had never been combat tested so their reliability and accuracy could not be depended upon.

While hopes of a supersonic B-52 replacement were revived after 1968 and potential successors, the Rockwell B-1B and Northrop Grumman B-2A Spirit, would be introduced, the B-52's versatility and low operating costs (only 25 percent of the B-2A's) would constantly appeal to the cost-cutters. Consequently, it survived in reduced numbers and will outlive its B-1B and B-2A replacements.

Soviet interceptors pursuing a *Chrome Dome* B-52H would have faced up to 1,200 rounds of 20mm fire from its General Electric M61A-1 rotary cannon, replacing the quad 0.5 or twin 20mm guns of previous B-52s. It was controlled by an Emerson AN/ASG-21 fire control system. (USAF)

CHRONOLOGY

1945

February At the Yalta Conference the Western Allies accept that Josef Stalin will dominate Eastern Europe. The partition of Germany into East and West is agreed six months later.

August Atomic bombs are dropped on Hiroshima and Nagasaki. Japan surrenders.

1946

March 5 Churchill declares that Soviet communism has lowered an "Iron Curtain" across Europe and avows that the USA and Britain must act as guardians of peace and stability.

March 21 The US Continental Air Forces are divided into three commands including Strategic Air Command (SAC) which was under the direct operational control of the US president.

July New US atomic tests over Bikini Atoll begin in Operation *Crossroads*.

1947

March 12 In the Truman Doctrine the US president resolves to limit communist expansion. The Marshall Plan, giving massive financial aid to rebuild Europe, is a tangible expression of US commitment, matched in theory by the Soviet Union's Molotov Plan.

December 17 The prototype Boeing XB-47 flies.

1948

September 19 Lt Gen Curtis LeMay takes over SAC from Gen George Kenney.

February Communist forces take control of Czechoslovakia.

June 24 Stalin begins the 11-month blockade of East Berlin. Warplan *Doublequick* includes heavy, conventional bombing of Soviet airbases by UK-based B-29s.

1949

April NATO is set up.

August 29 The USSR's first atomic bomb is built. Fears of a "nuclear Pearl Harbor" influence US defense policy, although Stalin does not include atomic weapons in Soviet defense plans.

1950

June Stalin supports and arms North Korea's invasion of South Korea. Communist China launches its own invasion force in November.

1951

April Gen Douglas MacArthur, leading Allied forces in Korea, is sacked for promoting the use of nuclear weapons against the communist forces and China.

1952

April 15 The YB-52 makes its first flight.

October 3 British atomic bomb tests begin.

October 31 In Operation *Ivy* the first hydrogen bomb ("Mike") is tested, destroying the island of Elugelab in the Marshall Islands with 700 times the power of the Hiroshima bomb.

December 16 The B-52A and RB-52B are ordered into production.

1953

July 27 An armistice ends the war in Korea.

August 12 Soviet atomic bomb tests begin.

B-47B-50-BW 51-2335 on the flight line. Whereas the B-47 design had relied largely on existing off-the-shelf equipment, the XB-52 was to be filled with innovative systems. (USAF)

1954

February Construction of the Distant Early Warning (DEW) line of 63 radar stations from Alaska to Greenland begins.

March US *Castle Bravo* hydrogen bomb tests take place at Bikini Atoll in the Marshall Islands producing a 15-megaton explosion.

1955

January 25 The first flight of the operational B-52B takes place.

May 14 The Warsaw Pact is formed, uniting military forces in Soviet countries.

June 29 The 93rd BW receives the first B-52B (52-8711) in service, flown to Castle AFB, California by Brig Gen William Eubank.

August Soviet hydrogen bomb tests begin, coupled with calls for a test ban treaty.

October SAC begins to evaluate quick-response ground alert for bombers.

1956

March 9 The B/RB-52C first flies.

May 14 The first B-52D flies. "Second source" B-52 production begins at the Wichita, Kansas facility.

May 21 A B-52B becomes the first aircraft to air-drop a thermonuclear bomb in Operation *Redwing-Cherokee.*

June 1956 The 42nd BW converts to B-52Bs as the second B-52 wing.

November 24–25 Operation *Quick Kick* demonstrates the B-52s' ability to reach the Soviet Union across the North Pole.

1957

January 16 Operation *Power Flite* takes three B-52Bs around the world with in-flight refueling on a 45-hour flight.

July 1 Gen Curtis LeMay hands control of SAC to Gen Thomas S. Power, regarded as the architect of *Chrome Dome* operations.

July Ground alert tests begin, using UK-based B-47 bombers.

August 26 The first Soviet ICBM, the SS-6 *Sapwood* with a 6,000-mile range, is tested.

October 1 SAC ground alert begins.

October 3 The first B-52E flies.

October 4 The Soviet Sputnik satellite is launched.

1958

May 6 The first B-52F flies, followed by the first B-52G on August 31.

July–August SAC units are placed on alert when a Soviet invasion of Lebanon is feared.

September 15 The first airborne alert tests begin, using the 42nd BW in *Head Start 1.*

1959

February 13 The B-52G enters service with the 5th BW. The USA now has 15,000 nuclear weapons in its arsenal.

December 21 The North American AGM-28 Hound Dog ALCM enters SAC service.

1960

May 1 Francis Gary Powers' U-2 reconnaissance aircraft is shot down over Russia. The US Navy launches its first nuclear-capable Polaris submarine.

SAC achieves its goal of having one-third of its bombers on 30-minute alert (reduced to 15 minutes when Soviet ballistic missiles are introduced).

June SAC tests the dispersal of its B-47 assets to smaller military and civilian bases.

July 20 The first B-52H flies.

August The Convair B-58A enters service.

November 8 John F. Kennedy becomes US president.

1961

January 18 Gen Power announces that SAC has flown 6,000 airborne alert sorties. They are christened *Chrome Dome* November 6 and last for seven years.

Operation *Hard Head* begins, monitoring the Thule Ballistic Missile Early Warning System (BMEWS) radar site.

January 24 The Goldsboro *Broken Arrow* incident occurs.

February Operation *Looking Glass* begins.

Early 1961 The McDonnell ADM-20 Quail decoy enters service.

March 14 The second *Broken Arrow* incident occurs at Yuba City, California.

May 9 The B-52H enters service with the 379th BW.

A 4136th SW B-52H makes a record 12,532-mile unrefueled flight, demonstrating its increased range.

July 1 SIOP-62, the first Single Integrated Operational Plan for nuclear warfare, is adopted.

August 12 Construction of the wall to seal off East Germany begins.

1962

July In Operation *Anadyr*, Khrushchev begins shipping missiles and personnel to Cuba.

October Soviet missiles in Cuba are photographed by a U-2. A naval blockade of Cuba begins on October 23.

B-52D 56-0591 *Tommy's Tigator* was used by the 4925th Test Group for nuclear weapon tests in Operation *Hardtack* at Eniwetok Island from April to August 1958, when the aircraft was commanded by Capt "Tommy" Summer. It was lost on June 23, 1959 with five Boeing employees during tests to assess airframe durability in flights below 500ft altitude. Failure of the horizontal stabilizer in turbulent conditions was blamed. (USAF)

On October 28 Khrushchev agrees to remove the missiles and nuclear-capable Il-28 bombers. The blockade is lifted.

October 26 The final B-52 is delivered, B-52H 61-040 for the 4136th SW at Minot AFB, North Dakota.

1963

July 25 The USSR, UK, and USA agree a partial atmospheric nuclear test ban.

November 22 President F. Kennedy is assassinated.

1964

August The Gulf of Tonkin incident accelerates US involvement in Vietnam.

October 16 China detonates a nuclear device.

December 1 Gen John D. Ryan takes over from Gen Thomas S. Power as SAC commander.

B-47 *Reflex* operations are ended.

1965

Bomber versions of the B-47 and the B-52B are retired.

December Secretary of Defense Robert McNamara announces a B-52 phase-out plan, reducing the fleet from 600 to 402 by the end of 1972.

1966

January 17 The Palomares *Broken Arrow* incident occurs.

1967 Israel's victory in the Six-Day War means intervention by the USA and the Soviet Union is avoided.

June 17 China explodes its first thermonuclear weapon.

1968

January 21 The Thule, Greenland *Broken Arrow* incident occurs, prompting the end of *Chrome Dome* and *Hard Head* operations.

1991

September 28 SAC nuclear ground alert aircraft are stood down.

ATTACKER'S CAPABILITIES

Developing a Cold War strategy

First steps

Operation *Chrome Dome* was in many ways a culmination of US defense policies which derived from the Soviet Union's supposed superiority in bomber and missile strength. Gen Thomas S. Power, among other influential generals, suggested early in 1960 that the Eisenhower administration had underestimated the Soviet nuclear threat and its supposed numerical superiority over SAC's resources. In fact, Eisenhower's doubts about Soviet capability, based partly upon the lack of suitable bomber airfields in northern Russia, were fully justified. However, he was aware of the likelihood of a Soviet hydrogen bomb and future delivery systems for it, so he commissioned the Surprise Attack Panel of experts to estimate the risk.

By 1961, one-third of USAF manpower was within SAC control, and in 1962 it had a record number of 282,723 personnel under its control. B-52 numbers peaked at over 600 aircraft between 1962 and 1964, reducing to 500 in 1969. Unlike other aspects of USAF organization, SAC was headed by a single person rather than several theater commanders. (USAF)

The resultant Killian Report ("Meeting the Threat of Surprise Attack"), published in February 1955 by the USAF's Science Advisory Panel, exacerbated US alarm at the supposed "bomber gap," the supposed numerical superiority of Soviet bomber forces to those of the USA. It suggested that the Soviet threat was far greater than planners had assumed and that there would be over 1,000 nuclear-capable bombers in Soviet service by 1959. The eventual revelation via U-2 surveillance from 1956 that this was a fallacy generated understandable opposition to the rapid expansion of US offensive capability. However, forceful proponents of airpower such as Gen LeMay were still able to preserve contracts for the "big bomber" programs in place and introduce improved B-52 versions.

With considerable prescience, the report advocated far-reaching measures that included dispersing America's bomber fleet and keeping some of the bombers flying on constant airborne alert, an idea supported by Gen LeMay but executed by Power. It recommended the development of land- and sea-based intermediate ballistic missiles and an antimissile system to intercept incoming Russian ICBMs.

Following that report, the same scientific advisors, led by James R. Killian, recommended the development of ICBMs and better means of gathering intelligence, using satellites. Thermonuclear warheads had become small enough to fit into ballistic missile warheads.

Killian also promoted the Lockheed U-2 and high-definition land reconnaissance cameras, both projects being handled in great secrecy by the CIA to avoid political clashes over funding. Much of the apparatus of the developing Cold War was therefore planned out in the 1950s, including the B-52 bombers which were in production.

Cold warriors

By April 1956, the Joint Chiefs of Staff (JCS) had persuaded Eisenhower to make massive increases in the defense budget, which included far more B-52s than he thought necessary. In October 1957, the launch of the Soviet satellite Sputnik 1, together with claims of successful Russian ICBM tests and the introduction of additional long-range nuclear-capable bomber types, presented further anxiety for American defense chiefs. Although Kennedy's Secretary of Defense Robert McNamara was able to dismiss the "missile gap" as a myth by February 1961 it enabled SAC, in the long term, to continue to establish a huge fleet of up to 2,500 strategic bombers. By 1959, Army Chief of Staff Gen Maxwell Taylor was able to tell the House of Representatives that the USA had enough nuclear weapons to destroy the Soviet Union ten times over: the so-called "overkill" advantage.

Rather than attempting to construct a perfect air defense system, it was acknowledged that if even one of the supposedly vast fleet of Soviet bombers could penetrate US defenses in a surprise attack and drop a nuclear bomb, the results would be catastrophic. Missiles launched offshore from Russian submarines would have given only a few minutes' warning. In the absence of a pre-prepared alert nuclear force of bombers, there would have been inadequate time to launch a retaliatory attack. The policy of nuclear deterrence could only be maintained with alert status providing the ability to deliver quick retaliation.

LeMay, tacitly acknowledging in 1957 that few of his aircraft would be able to take off by the time any Soviet intruders were detected by the radar chain, stated that his unofficial personal policy was to attack the enemy bases before the bombers got off the ground, relying on his "own intelligence" to know when that was necessary. It was a presumptuous statement, but the temptation to make a pre-emptive strike and avoid the consequences of an initial enemy attack was always present in both sides' planning throughout the Cold War. Le May's successor, Gen Power, was even more in favor of an SAC "first strike." *Chrome Dome* airborne alert improved the chances of making a calculated, neutralizing assault. However, the chances of fatal mistakes occurring in such a hair-trigger situation were considerable, despite all the safety measures in place.

The DEW line

Early warning of potential attacks was clearly a priority, so defense planners completed the *Pinetree* line of radar bases by 1952 and the Distant Early Warning (DEW) radar chain in 1957, which was over-flown several times by Soviet airliners making "navigational errors." They were all linked to the complex Semi-Automatic Ground Environment (SAGE) network that coordinated fighters and other air defense systems via its 275-ton computer complex, with 58,000 vacuum tubes and its own four-storey building. Together, they provided in-depth radar coverage across the whole of northern North America, theoretically providing sufficient time to alert fighters to incoming bombers and launch retaliatory bombing sorties.

From 1957, when the Soviet Union acquired ICBMs, the warning time was reduced to a few minutes. The ultimate solution, in Cold War logic, was to keep bombers in the air, ready to support US missiles in delivering retaliatory strikes. Within the 30-minute flight-time of a Soviet R-7 Semyorka missile, it was hoped that other aircraft would also be able to evacuate their bases before the missiles struck. Later, the satellite-based Missile Defense Alarm System (MIDAS), which was built to detect missiles through their infra-red signatures, was tested.

Communications between the North American Air Defense Command (NORAD), buried deep in Cheyenne Mountain, Colorado, and other elements in the defense net throughout most of the Cold War were made via the commercial telephone system. An extra 30 minutes' warning of missile attacks from the Atlantic was provided by a chain of radar "Texas Towers" planted offshore. One, Texas Tower 4, was swept away in a January 1961 storm together with its occupants.

In February 1961 the complex Ballistic Missile Early Warning System (BMEWS) was established at Thule AB, Greenland with other associated radar sites at Clear, Alaska and Fylingdales Moor in the UK. This radar chain was operated by NORAD in conjunction with Canada. Its 160ft tall antennae could track Soviet missiles at a 3,000-mile range. It was intended to give 15 minutes' warning of incoming ICBMs approaching from the north to allow SAC time to launch alert bombers and release its missiles. The launch "time window" at the northern Loring AFB, Maine B-52 base was less, only 11 minutes 40 seconds, while the more southerly Homestead, Florida had 19 minutes 30 seconds to launch its aircraft. The threat of off-shore submarine-launched missiles from the early 1960s curtailed even that small advantage.

The size of SAC's new bomber required elaborate equipment for maintainers to reach its extremities. B-52B-030-BO 53-0387 was an early delivery to the 93rd BW at Castle AFB in June 1956. The white fairing above the tail guns covered their General Electric MD-5 fire control system. Some B-52Bs had twin M-24A-1 20mm tail guns, like the B-47, in place of the four 0.50 M-3 guns with the A-3A fire control system that equipped most B-52A/B/C versions. (USAF)

Ground alert

SAC's newly instated 24-hour ground alert policy was first tested in Operation *Open Mind* in February 1955 with six 2nd BW B-47s of the 2nd BW loaded with Mk 6 nuclear training bombs. Crews were given 30 minutes' notice of briefing. They then started their engines and taxied to take off until the exercise was canceled. Armament crews practiced arming and disarming the bombs (the IFI/IFE cycle). These exercises were extended to all SAC bomber and tanker units from October 1,1957. The 2nd and 308th BWs at Hunter AFB, Georgia conducted Operation *Try Out* in which one-third of its B-47s had to be on alert status for five months in 1957. It included four no-notice launches of 44 bombers and revealed the enormous workload required for such a sustained effort. The similar Operations *Watch Tower* and *Fresh Approach* involved the 348th BW and 9th SBW respectively, leading to an Outstanding Unit Award for the 9th SBW at Mountain Home AFB. Ground alert would continue for 29 years.

Gen Power revealed the status of the alert force in November 1957 after B-36s were put on alert at Biggs AFB, Texas. It began as an occasional two or three-day commitment, but gradually developed into a regular routine of seven-day "confinements" to a purpose-built alert facility. By July 1960, it had been imposed to the point where one-third of SAC was put on 15-minute ground alert. Alert aircraft were fueled, armed, and pre-flighted. The jarring sound of the klaxon, followed by an alpha-numeric message ordering crews to their aircraft,

Take-off at maximum load of 488,000lb was among the most difficult stages of a mission. The main hazards were loss of an engine, or failure of the water injection system which pumped 10,000lb of demineralized water into the compressors within 110 seconds to increase the air density inside the engine. It added almost the equivalent power of two more engines, but it could be unreliable. The system was deleted in the more powerful turbofan engine B-52H, allowing more fuel tankage. (USAF)

soon became basic to life in SAC, but the tensions inherent in prolonged alert assignments caused many to resign.

Fast take-off times were clearly needed. For minimum interval take-off (MITO, pronounced "mee-toe"), bombers taxied out of their ten circular dispersal areas, arranged like a Christmas tree attached to the main runways. They accelerated straight onto the runway to very strict timings and took to the air in a continuous stream at 12- to 15-second intervals. They were staggered left, center and right across the runway to reduce the jet wash effect of aircraft ahead, although the last crews had to penetrate an accumulated haze of smoke and hot vapor from earlier take-offs as well as a heated runway, which extended the final jet's lift-off time. Visibility for aircraft towards the end of the queue could be less than 200ft. The slower-accelerating KC-135As would be included at 30-second intervals. On lift-off the bombers banked 15 degrees left or right alternately to avoid the turbulence, ready to join in a correctly spaced three-ship "cell." On good days, with exact timing, it was possible to get all 16 bombers and tankers in the air within eight minutes.

As Col Phil Rowe pointed out, "You hope that the fellows in front of you don't have a problem, for if they blow a tire, lose engines or otherwise slow down unexpectedly, you've got a real problem. That's why it's pucker time for everyone except the lead ship." Alert aircraft, as Col Mike Loughran explained, had cartridge starting systems installed in their number 4 and 6 engines (inboard pair) rather than using an external air starter. "With numbers 4 and 6 spooling up a selector was moved to the 'ground start' position after which the throttles were advanced to a high rpm [about 85 percent] to provide bleed air [through ducts] to the remaining six engines, although these could be started with just one running engine. It took a lot of power to get a 500,000lb B-52H moving, especially in the winter with the weight of the jet flattening the tires. Sometimes the tires even froze to the ground or to the chocks, which would then become jammed in front of your tires. It could be a real chore to break free. One technique was to try to rock the jet out by adding power and then chopping the throttles. If it was an all-out event you just added enough power to taxi right over them."

B-52D-060-BO 55-0093 on its delivery flight to the 42nd BW at Loring AFB, Maine in February 1967. Its short career ended on July 29, 1958 when it struck the ground three miles south of the runway on approach to Loring in poor visibility. (USAF)

The *Quick Start* project enabled all eight engines to be started at once. Engine start time was reduced from four minutes in cold weather to around 30 seconds. Misfired cartridges could be fire hazards, however. *Quick Start* also meant extra jobs for the ground crew, as Sgt Ken Kimmons recalled: "You had to clean eight breeches, transfer tubes and breach caps, then load each tube with a new cartridge every time you had an exercise. Then you had to reload the storage racks in the wheel wells with eight new cartridges in their cans."

For take-off the pilot advanced all eight throttles assisted by the co-pilot who checked that none of them slipped back from the maximum setting. With take-off weights exceeding 480,000lb the aircraft often needed most of the 13,500ft standard SAC runway. A 1.5-mile run before breaking ground would be typical for a *Chrome Dome* B-52D.

If the aircraft was unable to gain more than 400ft of altitude on take-off, the downward-ejecting seats for the two navigators could not be used as their parachutes had no time to open. In an emergency, it was impossible to jettison fuel. It had to be burned off while the jet orbited with its spoilers at maximum extension to increase drag. However, there were several cases of successful take-offs with failed engines. In one 1958 incident a 99th BW B-52B got airborne after losing three engines on one side. It climbed to 500ft and returned for a landing, losing two more on the right wing and touching down with only three working.

Take-off was preceded by the wing tips, which drooped on the ground, rising 30ft to the "flying" position. At 100ft altitude, the pilot raised the four landing-gear "trucks" and the two outrigger units supporting the wing tips. Flaps were raised to 15 percent. When the water injection system ran dry, noise was reduced, as were the characteristic plumes of smoke and water vapor following the bomber.

B-47E-65-LM 53-1884 blasts off for a 1957 ground alert sortie

The bomber's J35 engines left it seriously under-powered until the J47 engine became available for the B-47E version. In service, it acquired an unenviable reputation for very difficult handling, poor engine response, and a tendency to spin or stall. It also lacked all-weather bombing equipment, and its use as a low-altitude bombing system (LABS) bomber, requiring a high-g climb and half-loop to deliver a nuclear weapon, induced metal fatigue. One wing, the 306th BW, lost seven B-47s while practicing this manoeuvre and 251 were written off in accidents. During the 1956 Suez Crisis over 1,000 US-based B-47s flew simulated nuclear strike flights totaling 8 million miles over the Arctic zone and the USA. Although not an airborne alert like the later *Chrome Dome* missions, it showed that any potential threat could be faced quickly, albeit at tremendous operational expense.

1884
U.S. AIR FORCE

0-31884
884

The innovative computer technology that was entering SAC usage could cause problems for B-52 maintainers. Former 68th BW(H) crew chief Sgt Ken Kimmons recalled one SAC-wide false alarm: "I was on nuclear alert with my plane and the computer tech at NORAD HQ had done some repairs and was testing the computer system. He decided to run some sort of tape through the computer without telling the computer it was only a test. The klaxon went off in the middle of the night and we all came running out of the alert facility. There were no staff cars and no fire trucks! We got to the aircraft and got 'cranked up.' The pilot said 'Ground, disconnect interphone and remove wheel chocks. This is NOT a drill.' We all did as we were told and waited off the left wing for the plane to start rolling. We also kept an eye on the horizon, waiting for the sky to turn orange from the incoming warheads entering the atmosphere. After what seemed like a long time the cockpit light switched from red to white, which was my signal to return to the aircraft. You do not easily forget something like that!" Being on short-notice alert status did at least rule out major maintenance requirements, but routine tasks included "draining surge tanks, servicing LOX, and rotating tires so that they did not develop flat spots due to the weight of the aircraft and its load."

McNamara's budget-cutting strategy was emphasized in December 1961 when he declared that "as the number of [US] ballistic missiles increases, requirements for strategic aircraft will be gradually reduced. Simultaneously, the growing enemy missile capability will make grounded aircraft more vulnerable to sudden attack and further measures will have to be taken to increase the survivability of the strategic bomber force." Airborne alert was already established as one of the primary measures, although in November 1965 McNamara would attempt to cancel it as being "no longer necessary" after the introduction of the Minuteman ICBM. SAC won that debate.

Questions were also raised about the need to spend huge amounts on interceptor fighters. The problem had been highlighted in July 1953 when, in a "war game," 99 SAC bombers made a mass attack on several US cities and only two were "shot down" by Air Defense Command interceptors before reaching their targets. Following British Prime Minister Stanley Baldwin's 1932 assertion that "the bomber will always get through," SAC's (and the USAF's) preferred response was to accelerate production and development of its own bombers and missiles as a deterrent. There is little reason to assume that the Soviet air defenses would have done any better in July 1953, but experts, including the influential RAND think tank, spoke of unheralded attacks by hundreds of Tu-4 bombers which would drop atom bombs from 20,000ft, devastating air bases in the USA, Europe, and North Africa.

Hound Dog

On February 13, 1959, the B-52G, with a redesigned, shorter vertical stabilizer, was launched at Travis AFB, California with the 5th BW. It became the most widely used Stratofortress variant, offering an average range increase from 6,000 to 10,000 miles. Extra fuel totaling 41,000lb was carried in internal and external wing tanks, which helped to stabilize the wing in flight. Its lighter "wet" wing structure sustained various structural weaknesses early in the B-52G's career, requiring a $219m modification program. It proved to be less easy to handle than "tall tail" B-52s, because the ailerons had been removed and wing controls relied on seven sets of spoilers per wing. Many pilots preferred ailerons as spoilers, which when used insensitively could induce "Dutch roll." An electro-optical viewing system was installed beneath the nose from 1972 to provide steerable television (STV) and forward-looking infra-red (FLIR) views of the situation ahead of the bomber.

B-52Gs were also designed to carry the North American Aviation AGM-28 Hound Dog supersonic, jet powered, stand-off cruise missile, which was intended to take out static air defense sites and fighter bases with a one megaton W28 warhead ahead of a US nuclear strike.

The Hound Dog's jet engine could provide extra thrust for take-off, risking foreign object damage to its low-slung power-plant. Its fuel could be replenished in flight from the B-52's tanks. Its efficiency was demonstrated on April 12, 1960 when an Operation *Blue Nose* B-52G launched a Hound Dog at the end of a 20.5-hour flight to the North Pole and back at temperatures below –75°F. Hound Dog was used until 1975. (USAF)

Capt Robert Newton recalled: "The co-pilot started the [missile's] engine on the ground and kept it in 'idle' for electrical power to the missile for the entire mission. Programming was relatively easy once you had got all the initial information entered. After that you picked out radar points and used the bombing crosshairs to update its position. We were able to 'score' them by making a simulated launch and letting the missile guide just as if we were making a simulated bomb-run. Every unit with Hound Dogs had to make an annual live launch at Eglin AFB. As far as I was concerned, for its time it was a wonderful thing to work with."

Lt Col Don Campbell pointed out that, "We flew with it a lot and because we trained with it so much I really think we just wore them out. I remember saying that we screwed up the Hound Dog by flying it all the time and I was told that this was recognized and it was not going to happen with the ALCM [AGM-86A missile]."

SAC intended to replace Hound Dog missiles, after 15 years of service, with the Douglas GAM-87 Skybolt, which had a much longer range and a similar W59 nuclear warhead to the Minuteman ICBMs'. B-52H bombers could release it over 900 miles from a target, possibly beyond the borders of a hostile country. President Kennedy secured funding for the project to extend the life of the B-52 force, but successive test failures and the development of the Polaris SLBM brought about Skybolt's cancelation in 1962.The move also had profound consequences for the UK's nuclear bomber force, for which the British Blue Streak missile had already been canceled in favor of Skybolt. Many felt that the cancelation was part of an American policy to reduce the UK's role in a nuclear partnership with the USA, but Kennedy agreed to supply the submarine-launched Polaris missile instead.

Quail

In 1960, the B-52G wings also began to receive the McDonnell GAM-72A (ADM-20) Quail jet-powered decoy drone. Dropped from a B-52's bomb-bay it carried radar reflectors which gave enemy early warning radars the same signature as a full-sized B-52. Eight could be carried, although the normal load was two, with a "clip" of four standard, silver B28

A GAM-72A Quail is launched from B-52D-040-BW 56-6695. Quail may have been effective against radars and fighters, but it would not have decoyed the more advanced Soviet ground-to-air missiles. Large numbers of bombers and Quails could, however, have swamped the early warning radars. (US Government)

hydrogen bombs occupying the rest of the bomb bay and usually fused at 1.1 megatons each. Quail remained in service until 1978 when it became clear that air-launched cruise missiles, such as the supersonic AGM-69A SRAM, would allow B-52s to launch attacks from outside the enemy's air defense zone.

Tanking

In-flight refueling was key to all alert operations, including *Chrome Dome.* Keeping a dozen B-52s aloft for a day required the transfer of 654,000 gallons of aviation fuel each day. In-flight refueling was considered to be the most demanding feature of most B-52 flights, requiring considerable piloting skills and fraught with danger of a mid-air collision. Eleven B-47 and B-52 bombers were lost during in-flight refueling, but the B-52 and its essential KC-135 tanker were an integral double act in the Cold War drama. Boeing's K-135A, developed at the same time as the company's 707 airliner, originated from company jet transport studies in 1946 at a time when the jet engine already had a poor reputation for reliability and excessive fuel consumption. When the B-52 design was revised in 1948 to have eight turbojets and its overall weight increased considerably, the need for a dedicated tanker became urgent.

Funding limits initially precluded a replacement for SAC's 800 piston-engine KC-97s and a tanker conversion of the B-47 was suggested as a cheaper option. Boeing forged ahead with design ideas for a company-funded transport/tanker/airliner powered by four J57 engines (the same as the B-52A's) to be ready within two years of the XB-52's first flight on April 15, 1952. The prototype of the Model 367-80, as it was originally known, was rolled out on May 15, 1954 in the hope that the USAF would fund a tanker version, also allowing Boeing to win greater success than it had previously enjoyed in the civil aviation market.

Gen LeMay saw the logic in acquiring tankers that could match the B-52s' performance on their extended nuclear strike missions. In November 1953 he requested 200 jet tankers, leading to an evaluation of the idea by the Wright Air Development Center. Although the USAF held a design competition for the aircraft, the Boeing design was clearly ahead in development and the favorite with SAC leaders. Continued contractual arguments over costs and the separation of military KC-135A and civilian B-707 production persisted until the roll-out of the first KC-135A Stratotanker on July 18, 1956, the same day as the last KC-97 left the production line.

Flight tests yielded very positive results, but they also revealed two problems that would affect the aircraft throughout its service career. The lack of power on take-off made the failure of an engine at that point an unrecoverable emergency. Inevitably, any crashes resulted in the loss of most crew members, as there were no means of escape. A 15 percent increase in engine power, through water injection into the engine compressors to reduce temperatures and allow higher revolutions, only partially alleviated the problem. Linked to this was the realization that the tanker could only operate from 13,500ft SAC runways rather than smaller forward bases. However, the KC-135A, which had over four times the fuel load of a KC-97, was vital to SAC's needs, so the first operational example was delivered to the 93rd Air Refueling Squadron at Castle AFB, California on June 28, 1957. In November, LeMay commanded a KC-135A on a record-breaking flight, Operation *Long Legs*, to and from Argentina and gave the Soviet Union another demonstration of SAC's intercontinental reach.

In service, SAC welcomed the tanker's ability to operate at the same speeds and altitudes as bombers. "Mating" took place at around 255kts after the B-52 pilot homed on to a "parrot" radar beacon signal emitted by the tanker, so then the bomber could take on around 125,000lb of fuel. One of the co-pilot's jobs was to manage the input of fuel into the tanks in a set sequence to preserve the aircraft's center of gravity, recording all the details in a fuel log. Fuel transfer between the wing tanks continued during the landing approach to keep the wings level for taxiing.

For a B-52 pilot, manipulating the eight throttles, the trim switches, and the wing spoilers to keep the heavy aircraft in position on a tanker required manual dexterity worthy of a

For decades, the KC-135A was an essential partner to the B-52. This KC-135A-06-BN began operations in December 1957, and it was still refueling B-52s in the 1990s. The importance of in-flight refueling was emphasized early on in 1954's Operation *High Gear*, in which KC-97s of the 22nd and 91st ARS performed 113 refuelings for B-47s deployed to Sidi Slimane in Morocco, showing that "air refueling for range extension of B-47s has been proven feasible under all conditions." (USAF)

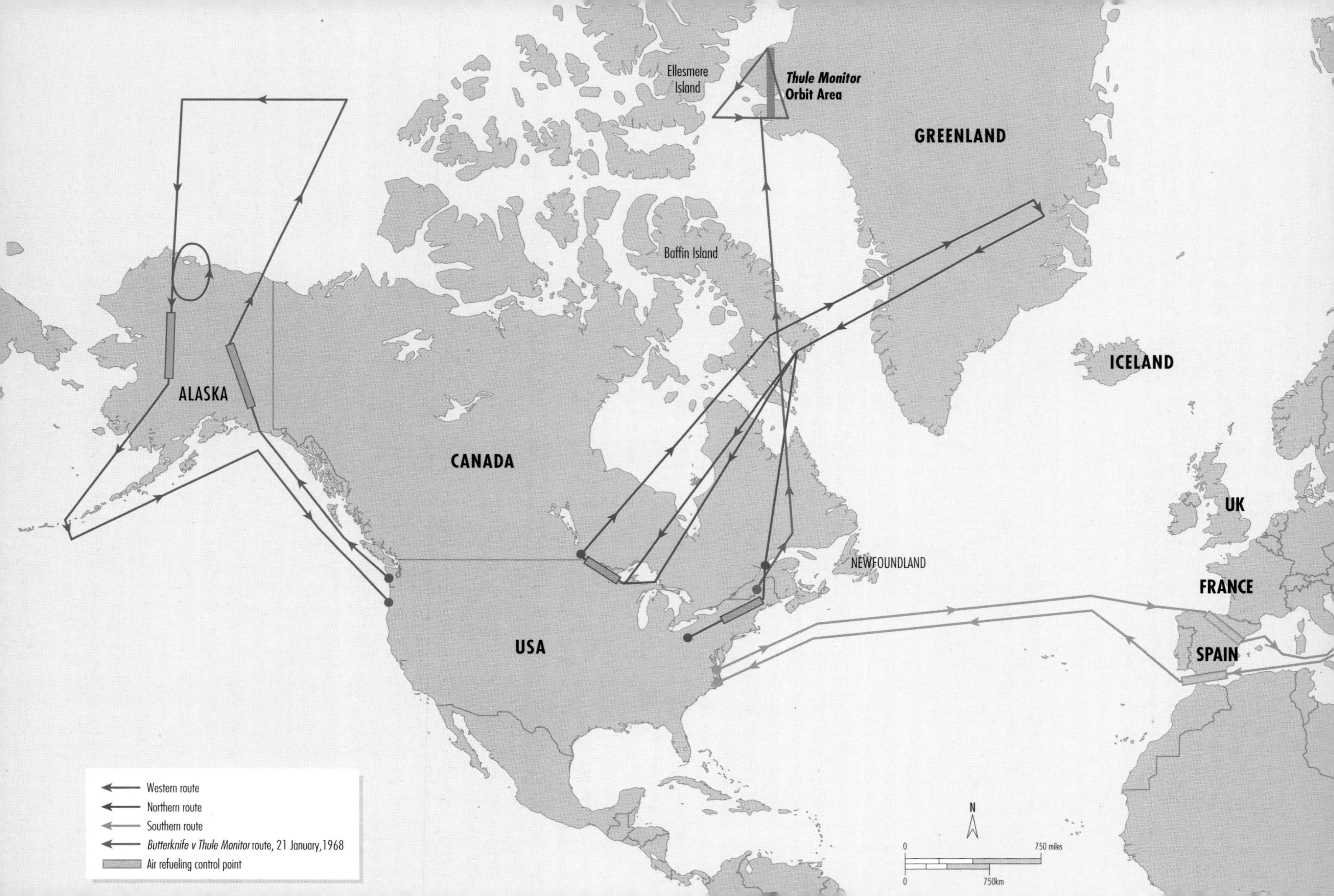
Thule Monitor
Orbit Area
Ellesmere
Island
GREENLAND
Baffin Island
ICELAND
ALASKA
CANADA
UK
NEWFOUNDLAND
FRANCE
USA
SPAIN
N
0
750 miles
0
750km
Western route
Northern route
Southern route
Butterknife v Thule Monitor route, 21 January, 1968
Air refueling control point

OPPOSITE OPERATION *CHROME DOME* AND *HARD HEAD (THULE MONITOR)* ROUTES 1966–68

In 1966, two flights per day were made on the western route, which involved airborne alert orbits over Alaska. Four flights covered the northern route from bases such as Wurtsmith AFB and K I Sawyer AB. Bombers and tankers from other bases would follow different routes. The southern (Mediterranean) route usually required six daily flights. The *Butterknife V Thule Monitor* route shown is the one followed on January 21 by B-52G 58-0188 Hobo 28 from the 380th BW at Plattsburgh AFB when it crashed on approach to Thule, Greenland, scattering radioactive material and bringing *Chrome Dome* to a close.

concert pianist for effective "spoiler flapping" (left and right spoilers extended alternately to reduce speed by up to 10kts) and physical stamina to hold the bomber steady for up to half an hour. On *Chrome Dome* missions the optimum time for this was 26 minutes. Quicker air refueling increased the bomber's range and opened up additional targets. Turbulence could cause disconnects from a tanker, depending on the dexterity of the pilots and "boomers." During an operational readiness inspection, crews were allowed three disconnects during a 15-minute refueling.

Crucially, the tankers could then operate from the same northern US bases as B-47s and B-52s, remaining on alert with the bomber crews and accompanying them on transit flights or on the outward section of their combat missions. If forward bases of the required size were available, the tankers could then refuel and fly to meet returning bombers. They could also be prepared to meet B-52s or B-58As coming from bases further south in the USA and refuel them. One tanker could fill up at least two B-52s with its 33ft-long "flying Boom" probe – a fully loaded B-52 could burn up to 20,000lb of fuel per hour. The maneuverability of the boom extended to 10 degrees each side of the centerline, 20 degrees above neutral and 40 degrees below it. Transferring 120,000lb without a disconnect from the tanker due to turbulence or error qualified the crew for "One Gulp Club" membership.

KC-135As were also based at Moron AB, Spain to refuel both *Reflex* B-47s and *Chrome Dome* B-52s. Col John Moser was a KC-135A navigator: "Most days we flew two missions a day, refueling the incoming airborne alert B-52s over the Mediterranean as they proceeded to their alert patterns off the coast of the Soviet Union." They were not always routine sessions. On one refueling, "we had the worst weather for that type of operation that I had ever flown in. The visibility was zero at our refueling altitude. Under any other circumstances, the mission would have been scrubbed but our designated B-52 was inbound and required fuel to complete its airborne alert mission. I picked up the bomber's beacon and gave him the weather situation; he proceeded toward our rendezvous point. The rendezvous was as perfect as any I have ever seen. Neither aircraft ever had visual contact with the other until the bomber 'slid' neatly under the rear of the tanker at 50ft and got ready to connect with the tanker boom for his fuel. I was convinced that night that if the electronics worked properly, we could rendezvous and refuel in any weather conditions."

Other tankers were positioned in Alaska and Newfoundland. The fueling requirements were formidable: Moron-based tankers were expected to deliver at least 205,000 gallons daily to *Chrome Dome* flights, while those in Alaska and other northern locations combined to pump 450,000 gallons into B-52s. The acquisition of KC-135s greatly increased SAC's flexibility and made possible both ground and air alert missions, including *Chrome Dome*. If bomber crews were given a positive Emergency Action Message "go code," their last refueling would take the majority of the tanker's fuel, leaving little for its own return trip.

Looking Glass

SAC's essential command and control facilities were inevitably targets for Soviet missiles or bombers. The main facility was in $9m, three-storey bunkers beneath the command's headquarters in Building 500 at Offutt AFB, Nebraska, but there were others at Barksdale,

OPPOSITE B-52 BASES AND UNITS IN THE USA

Additional bases outside the USA included Ramey AFB, Puerto Rico where the 72nd BW, 60th BS operated B-52Gs from August 1959 to June 1971 and 3rd Air Division base at Andersen AFB, Guam, which was extensively used by SAC B-52 units during the Vietnam War period and by the 43rd SW from 1972.

Louisiana, March AFB, California, and Westover AFB, Massachusetts. The loss of those centers would have meant that SAC was unable to fulfill its basic deterrent purpose with retaliatory strikes. A less vulnerable airborne command center was therefore necessary and it was clear that some of the nuclear strike force, including alternative command and control platforms, had to be in airborne or dispersed locations to escape destruction. Some EC-135A/G airborne command and control aircraft had airborne launch and control systems installed for the remote launching of ICBMs. This required two launch keys to be turned in unison from two separate launch consoles on receipt of orders from the president and the verification of classified launch codes. Practice launch missions were known as "glory trips." As LeMay pointed out in 1988, no ICBM with a nuclear warhead had ever been launched, so bombers still offered the best-known characteristics.

Boeing EC-135 electronic communications aircraft were vital to the airborne alert mission. Plans to use a C-135 variant as airborne command platforms originated in 1958 and a year's operational tests with a KC-135A (58-0022) began in May 1960 for the Airborne National Command Post project. From July 1960, five examples were placed at Offutt AFB, Nebraska on 15 minutes' alert with the 34th Air Refueling Squadron to orbit near the air base. Delegation of responsibility for ordering a nuclear strike if the president was incapacitated was a source of deep concern throughout the Cold War. If SAC HQ or other command posts were destroyed, an SAC colonel or general, the Airborne Emergency Action Officer, aboard the airborne command post would have assumed command of the forces required for a retaliatory strike, even to the extent of remotely launching Minuteman II ICBMs.

President Eisenhower allegedly organized, in great secrecy, a command structure to take over that responsibility in the event of the president and leaders empowered to sanction the use of nuclear weapons being killed or unable to communicate. Five "authorizing commanders" including the SAC commander and four other commanders in chief had that authority. "Go-codes" for bombers to attack their targets could be transmitted from the EC-135s if Offutt HQ, obviously a prime target, was hit. Eventually the fleet expanded to 20 airborne command posts supported by 36 relay station aircraft.

President Kennedy's 1961 flexible response policy required one of the aircraft, code-named *Looking Glass*, to indicate that their role "reflected" that of the SAC command center, to be airborne at any given time on an eight-hour sortie. Another ten aircraft were available on 15-minute alert from February 3, 1961. All bombers and tankers also had to be airborne within that time, so the first would have to lift off in less than eight minutes. This routine continued throughout the Cold War until July 24, 1990.

Nuclear attacks implied widespread electronic disruption of vital communications required to organize an effective response. In 1962, SAC reorganized and enlarged its arcane Post-Attack Command and Control System (PACCS) to include three auxiliary airborne command and control units with KC-135As, similarly equipped with *Looking Glass* aircraft. They were attached to tanker bases at Barksdale, Westover, and March, and four support squadrons. Other support squadrons at four bases operated EB-47Ls equipped to act as communications posts in PACCSs. They were replaced by EC-135s in 1965.

The first of four National Emergency Airborne Command Post (NEACP) KC-135As was delivered to the 1000th Airborne Command and Control Squadron (ACCS) at Andrews AFB in February 1962, increasing the number of command post aircraft to 16. In an emergency the president and other key officials would have been helicoptered from

Barksdale AFB, Louisiana.
4238th SW. 436th BS (B-52F August 1958-April 1963), **2nd BW**. 20th BS (B-52F April 1963-June 1965). 62nd BS B-52G (June 1965 – Dec 1992). 596th BS (B-52G April 1968-October 1992)

Travis AFB, California.
5th BW. 23rd BS (B-52G February 1959-July 1968), 31st BS (B-52G February 1959-January 1960)

Walker AFB, New Mexico.
6th BW. 24th BS (B-52E December 1957-January 1967), 39th BS (B-52E December 1957-January 1963), 40th BS (B-52E December 1957-January 1967)

Carswell AFB, Texas. **7th BW**. 9th BS (B-52E January 1958-June 1968), 20th BS (B-52F June 1965-June 1968), 492nd BS (B-52F June 1958-June 1959)

Altus AFB, Oklahoma.
11th BW. 26th BS (B-52E January 1958-July 1968), 42nd BS (B-52E January 1958-June 1960). 17th BW. 34th BS (B-52E February 1963-July 1968 at Wright-Patterson AFB), 19th BW. 28th BS (B-52H February 1962-July 1968 at Homestead AFB, Florida)

March AFB, California.
22nd BW. 2nd BS (B-52B September 1963-1966,B-52D 1966-October 1982), 486th BS (B-52D October 1966-July 1971, B-52E 1968-70)

Ellsworth AFB, South Dakota.
28th BW. 77th BS (B-52D June 1967-1971),717th BS (B-52D June 1957-February 1960), 718th BS (B-52D June 1957-February 1960)

Eglin AFB, Florida.
4135th SW. 301st BS (B-52G July 1959-February 1963), **39th BW**. 62nd BS (B-52G February 1963-June 1965)

Ellsworth AFB, Maine.
42nd BW. 69th BS (B-52G 1959-March 1994), 70th BS (B-52G 1959 -June 1966), 75th BS (B-52D 1957, October 1959)

10. **Seymour Johnson AFB**, North Carolina. **4241st SW**. 73rd BS (B-52G July 1959-April 1963), **68th BW**. 51st BS (B-52G April 1963-September 1982)
11. **Clinton-Sherman AFB**, Oklahoma.
4123rd SW. **98th BS**. (B-52E January 1958-February 1963), **70th BW**. 6th BS (B-52E February 1963-1968, B-52D 1968-December 1969)
12. **Glasgow AFB**, Montana.
4141st SW. 326th BS (B-52D April 1961-February 1963), **91st BW**. 322nd BS (B-52D February 1963-June 1968)
13. **Fairchild AFB**, Washington.
92nd BW. 325th BS (B-52D March 1957-1971), 326th BS (B-52D March 1957-April 1961), 327th BS (March 1957-June 1960)
14. **Castle AFB**, California.
93rd BW. 328th BS (B-52B June 1955-65, B-52D June 1956-58 and 1965-74, B-52E 1957-58 and 1967-70), 329th BS (B-52B June 1955-1965, B-52D June 1956-58 and 1965-71, B-52E 1957-58 and 1967-70, B-52F 1958-September 1971, B-52G 1966-67), 330th BS (B-52B June 1955-63, B-52D June 1956-58, B-52E 1957-58, B-52F 1958-63), 4017th CCTS (B-52B January 1955-56)
15. **Biggs AFB**, Texas. 95th BW.
334th BS (B-52B 1959-June 1966)
16. **Dyess AFB**, Texas.
96th BW. 337th BS (B-52E December 1963-1970, B-52D 1969-82)
17. **Blytheville AFB**, Arkansas.
97th BW. 340th BS (B-52G January 1960-1992)
18. **Westover AFB**, Massachusetts.
99th BW. 346th BS (B-52B 1958-59, B-52C December 1956-1971, B-52D 1957-61 and 1966-72), 347th BS (B-52B 1958-59, B-52C December 1956-71, B-52D 1957-61 and 1966-72), 348th BS (B-52B 1957-61, B-52C December 1956-71, B-52D 1957-61 and 1966-72)
19. **McCoy AFB**, Florida.
4047th SW. 347th BS (B-52D September 1961-April 1963), **306th BW**. 367th BS (B-52D April 1963-October 1973)
20. **Mather AFB**, California.
4134th SW. 72nd BS (B-52F October 1958-February 1963), **320th BW**. 441st BS (B-52F February 1963-1968, B-52G 1968-89)
21. **Bergstrom AFB**, Texas.
4130th SW. 335th BS (B-52D January 1959-September 1963), 340th BW. 486th BS (B-52D September 1963-October 1966
22. **Wurtsmith AFB**, Michigan.
379th BW. 524th BS (B-52H May 1961-1977)
23. **Plattsburgh AFB**, New York.
380th BW. 528th BS (B-52G June 1966-January 1971)
24. **Dow AFB**, Maine.
4038th SW. 341st BS (B-52G May 1960-February 1963), **397th BW**. 596th BS (B-52G February 1963-April 1968)
25. **K I Sawyer AFB**, Michigan.
4042nd SW. 526th BS (B-52H July 1961-February 1963), **410th BW**. 644th BS (B-52H February 1963-November 1994)
26. **Griffiss AFB**, New York.
4039th SW. 75th BS (B-52G January 1960-February 1963), **416th BW**. 668th BS (B-62G February 1963-1992)
27. **Kincheloe AFB**, Michigan.
4239th SW. 93rd BS (B-52H November 191-February 1963), **449th BW**. 716th BS (B-52H February 1963-September 1977)
28. **Minot AFB**, North Dakota.
4136th SW. 525th BS (B-52H July 1961-February 1963), **450th BW**. 720th BS (B-52H February 1963-July 1968), **5th BW** (23rd BS B-52H July 1968-current)
29. **Columbus AFB**, Mississippi.
4228th SW. 492nd BS (B-52F June 1959-February 1963), **454th BW**. 736th BS (B-52F February 1963-1966, B-52G 1966 July 1969)
30. **Beale AFB**, California.
4126th SW. **31st BS (B-52G January 1960-January 1963), 456th** BW. 744th BS (B-52G February 1963-September 1975)
31. **Amarillo AFB**, Texas.
4128th SW. 718th BS (B-52D February 1960-January 1963), **461st BW**. 764th BS (B-52D February 1963-March 1968)
32. **Larson AFB**, Washington.
4170th SW. 327th BS (B-52D June 1960-February 1963), **462nd SAW**. 768th BS (B-52E February 1963-April 1966)
33. **Robins AFB**, Georgia.
4137th SW, 342nd BS (B-52G August 1960-February 1963), **465th BW**. 781st BS (B-52G February 1963-July 1968)
34. **Turner AFB**, Georgia.
4138th SW. 336th BS (B-52D July 1959 February 1963), 484th BW. **824th BS** (B-52D February 1963-January 1967)
35. **Sheppard AFB**, Texas.
4245th SW. 717th BS (B-52D January 1960-January 1963), **494th BW**. 864th BS (B-52D February 1963-April 1966)
36. **Pease AFB**, New Hampshire.
509th BW. 393rd BS (B-52D April 1966-November 1969)
37. **Wright-Patterson AFB**, Ohio.
4043rd SW. 42nd BS (B-52E June 1960-February 1963)
38. **Grand Forks AFB**, North Dakota.
4133rd SW, 30th BS (B-52H April 1962-February 1963), **319th BW**. 46th BS (B-52H February 1963-1982, B-52G 1982-86)
39. **Boeing, Seattle**.

RB-52Bs were built alongside B-52Bs, with 27 within the B-52B contract for 50 aircraft. 53-0377 was delivered to the 93rd BW in June 1956 and later flew with the 95th, 99th and 306th BW before withdrawal for use as a ground instruction airframe at Andersen AFB in June 1966. (USAF)

Washington to Andrews AFB to board a *Night Watch* NEACP KC-135A and orbit at a safe distance to continue command. In January 1965 the aircraft were all redesignated EC-135As, or EC-135Cs in the case of those adapted from KC-135Bs, of which 17 more were delivered. From 1965 the EC-135 fleet was expanded, and new versions were developed for use outside the USA. RAF Mildenhall, England hosted four *Silk Purse* EC-135H command posts for the European theater and five *Blue Eagle* EC-135As went to Hickam AFB, Hawaii for the US Commander in Chief, Pacific. SAC's EC-135s were operated under the *Cover All* mission name. Five more EC-135Cs (and other variants) were based at Langley AFB with the 6th ACCS of the 1st Tactical Fighter Wing for use by the Atlantic Command.

If a national emergency occurred during the Cold War a *Looking Glass* EC-135 and two KC-135 Auxiliary Airborne Command Posts (AUXCP) would have flown designated orbits over the central USA while three 4th ACCS airborne launch control center (ALCC, "al-see") EC-135A/Gs were to patrol near the LGM-30 Minuteman ICBM bases in the northern parts of the continent, in case the missile control centers were hit. Additional radio relay EC-135Ls orbited over the western USA to maintain links with a *Night Watch* NEACP flying at a safe distance off the eastern coast. Battle staff aboard the *Looking Glass* aircraft were empowered to take control of the situation if contact with the NEACP was lost. They could direct the launching of SAC B-52s or, in the 1960s, command the *Chrome Dome* bombers that would already have been heading for their targets. They could also direct those B-52s to safe bases and refueling facilities on their return, as well as launching all the available ICBMs.

It was understood that communications with US units or US Navy missile-launching submarines could have been hampered by radiation-induced electromagnetic pulses, as would SAC's long-range single sideband (SSB) communications. In 1961, together with *Looking Glass*, the Air Force proposed some bizarre back-up devices for communications in extremis. Some were approved, including rockets launched from four sites around Omaha containing HF transmitters to send go-codes. The Earth Waves project also used the terrain to transmit low-frequency emergency signals.

DEFENDER'S CAPABILITIES

"Red alert"

Soviet offensive forces

The first Soviet air defense missile was the System-25 Berkut (Golden Eagle), Stalin's response to the bombing of North Korean cities by SAC B-29s. Devised by Semyon Lavochkin and Sergei Beria, the missile was to have equipped 56 regiments in defensive rings around Moscow. The hugely expensive system was active from June 1956, but it failed to detect any of the US reconnaissance flights that entered Moscow airspace, and it was obsolescent by 1957. (Leonidl/Wikipedia creative commons)

The USSR's acquisition of thermonuclear weapons in 1953 meant that a single bomber might penetrate US defenses and destroy a major city with one bomb. In retrospect, Soviet policy during the Cold War could be seen as defensive and reactive in its response to the growth of NATO strength, although the West generally assumed that the Soviet Union would have been the potential aerial attacker. Josef Stalin had always prioritized land forces over the development of airpower and the USSR's aircraft and missile programs post-1945 were instigated as responses to US increases in offensive capability. However, openly expansionist acts such as placing missiles on Cuban territory, the Berlin Crisis and the suppression of the Hungarian Revolution in 1956 were seen as direct threats to the West and reasons for it to increase defense spending. In the immediate postwar years there appeared to be no real threat of Soviet invasion or bomber attack, but Stalin had inveighed against "capitalist encirclement" of the Soviet Union which might well, in his plans, lead to war.

While the Allies were rapidly disbanding their World War II forces the Soviet Union kept 4.5 million troops and over 15,000 aircraft. A veil of secrecy descended over the Soviet bloc as the Iron Curtain made it more difficult for the West to gain information on Soviet military strength. The Soviet Union's acquisition of nuclear weapons through a spying campaign in 1949 changed the situation drastically and accelerated Western defense spending. Soviet atmospheric nuclear tests in 1956 and 1961 were monitored by filter-equipped "sniffer" *Sea Fish* 95th BW B-36s and 93rd BW B-52Fs, providing information on the progress of the Soviet nuclear program.

When, in 1955 President Eisenhower proposed "Open Skies", by which the West and the Soviet Union would allow mutual surveillance overflights to show their bases and defenses, Nikita Khrushchev saw it as a plot against the USSR which would only reveal the weakness of its military resources. Khrushchev, the Soviet Union's forceful and cunning leader, had become president of the Soviet Union in 1953. His increasingly vociferous nuclear threats and expenditure on prestigious projects such as the space program were partly designed

The USA would not supply Stalin with B-29s during World War II, but Tupolev OKB reverse-engineered one of the four that made emergency landings in the Soviet Union rather than proceeding with their Tu-10 bomber design. As the Tu-4, with Soviet Ash-73 engines and Nudelman 23mm guns, it provided the Soviet Union with its first operational long-range heavy bomber from 1949, and in China some examples remained in service until 1988. (Public Domain)

to promote economic attrition in the West by encouraging ever more extravagant defense spending, albeit at a considerable economic cost to the Soviet people. He funded the SS-6 *Sapwood* ICBMs, launched from hidden underground silos, although the technical problems of this program caused its cancelation in 1961. The fixed silo launching method was revived, however, and by 1976 75 percent of Soviet ICBMs was in them, making them static targets but hard to destroy. American nuclear forces were more widely dispersed.

In 1959 Khrushchev had reduced the 5 million-strong Soviet Army by 20 percent, stating that nuclear missiles, rather than costly conventional forces, should provide the nation's defenses. In his estimation this gave the USSR parity with the USA, disguised technical and logistical shortcomings in his military, and increased Soviet pride and assertiveness on the world stage. Politically, after World War II, he could rely on his people's deep-seated and enduring hatred and suspicion of the West. In the mid-1950s, he portrayed his empire as being surrounded by American airbases and threatened by US Jupiter missiles based in Italy and Turkey. His possession of nuclear-capable ICBMs and bombers encouraged Khrushchev to threaten other world leaders, both privately and in public speeches, with imminent annihilation. Citing the United States' use of atom bombs to end the war with Japan, he persuaded Russians that those attacks were actually intended as threats of future devastation of the Soviet Union.

The belligerent comments of United States Gen Douglas MacArthur, who had advocated using nuclear weapons against North Korea and China in 1951, fed into this narrative. By 1960, Khrushchev's increasingly bellicose comments and robust responses from Adm Arthur Radford, chairman of the JCS, and from Gen LeMay asserting the United States' nuclear supremacy, increased public awareness worldwide that a nuclear war was perhaps imminent.

By 1954, the USSR was thought to have over 1,200 bombers in a force accustomed to flying in Arctic and North Atlantic areas, while SAC had 1,765 in its inventory. In October 1957, the launch of the Soviet satellite Sputnik 1, although without direct military significance, together with claims of successful ICBM tests and the introduction of long-range nuclear-capable bombers, appeared to give Soviet forces a clear lead. They undermined the United States' self-confidence and revived Pearl Harbor-type fears. A $40 billion civil defense and bomb shelter building program was proposed by the US government, based on exaggerated estimates of the USSR's bomber and missile capability, but it was rejected by Eisenhower as a panicky measure. However, President Kennedy had to introduce a similar plan during the 1962 Berlin Wall Crisis when a nuclear duel with the Soviet Union was threatened and Khrushchev boasted of a 100-megaton bomb that could be launched at the United States in a missile.

Khrushchev was aware that hawks such as LeMay in the USA would demand massive defense budget increases and that the supposed "missile gap" between US and USSR ICBM arsenals, allegedly underplayed and underfunded by Eisenhower, was used by Kennedy as an election ploy in 1960. Many in government felt that the USSR's apparently unrestricted defense spending would enable it to overtake even SAC's mighty resources. In fact, many Soviet generals in the 1950s saw that the USA had far superior reserves of both nuclear and conventional weapons and forecast little prospect of being able to attack the United States. Their strategic aims were directed far more towards Europe with American bases and missile installations as primary targets.

Soviet weapons

Andrei Tupolev reverse-engineered the B-29, several of which were interned in the USSR during World War II. The cloned version was the Tu-2 Bull and 857 were produced up to 1952 as Russia's first intercontinental bomber. That experience assisted in the production

The P-14 *Tall King* long-range early warning VHF radar threatened US bombers from 1959 until 1982. Usually operated from static locations with a crew of five, it was also available in a cumbersome transportable version that took 24 hours to assemble. Upgraded versions remain in service in other countries. (Wiki/ShinePhantom)

A preserved example of the Myasishchev M-4 Molot (Bison) strategic bomber, designed to deliver nuclear weapons to US mainland targets. Its appearance at the 1954 Soviet May Day flypast caused alarm in the United States and appeared to justify large orders for B-47 and B-52 bombers in response. (Wiki/Mike1979Russia)

of the larger Tu-95 Bear, which had the same wing-sweep as the B-52 but used turbo-prop engines. Like the B-52, its longevity in service throughout the Cold War and into the 21st century derives from its adaptability to new weapons such as cruise missiles, which were used extensively against Ukraine in 2022.

Most of the Cold War Soviet bombers and missiles were for medium-range attacks, not intercontinental use. The Tu-95 was vulnerable to interceptors and surface-to-air missiles and the Myasishchev M-4 Bison, with unreliable jet engines, lacked the range for a two-way attack on the USA. Khrushchev later admitted that "America itself was beyond our reach." In 1954, the jet-powered Tu-16 Badger was introduced to rival US jet bombers and 1,500 were built, but its 1,100-mile tactical radius limited it to potential European targets. A high subsonic maximum speed, powerful 21,000lb thrust engines, and the ability to carry AS-1 stand-off missiles made it a versatile aircraft that remained in service until 1993.

In February 1954, details were published in the USA of the Myasishchev M-4 Molot (Bison-A) bomber which was thought capable of delivering nuclear weapons to the US land mass. In fact, its 5,000-mile range was inadequate for flights to heartland targets from Soviet bases, although the appearance of 28 M-4s overflying the Tushino Aviation Day in Moscow in July 1955, viewed by an American air attaché, persuaded the CIA that this fleet could quickly expand to include several hundred examples. It was revealed, years later, that the same group of ten M-4s had overflown the display twice, adding eight more on its second pass. Only 93 examples were ever manufactured and less than 20 were nuclear capable, but the Kremlin boasted that over 400 were in service.

The West lacked information on the true situation in the early 1950s, partly because the CIA, under Allen Dulles, distrusted intelligence acquired by technical means, preferring to rely on old-fashioned spying, which had become virtually impossible in the USSR. However, Soviet self-aggrandizing propaganda promoted faster production of B-52s and the development of more capable air defense fighters. In 1950, USAF Chief of Staff Hoyt Vandenberg had stated that existing air defenses could destroy no more than a third of incoming Soviet bombers.

The true size of the Soviet bomber force was revealed when CIA reconnaissance flights by U-2s began in July 1956. The first of these detected 30 M-4s on an airfield near Leningrad, leading to the assumption that there would be many more at other bases. In fact, this fleet comprised the entire Bison "herd" at the time. Surveillance of the likely production centers over the following two years by U-2 pilots showed that Bison manufacture had actually slowed down. By 1963 it had ended.

Soviet defenses

By the mid-1960s, Soviet defensive assets had steadily expanded to include over 2,000 radar sites with 6,000 radar units and a distant warning line of 187 giant P-14 *Tall King-A* VHF radars operating at a 400-mile range. Many sites incorporating powerful jammers and other electronic countermeasures to defeat B-52 radars ringed the vast Soviet empire. B-52 electronic warfare officers (EWs) required expert knowledge of all these threats. Soviet radar operators knew that many potential targets were on the Soviet West Front, Murmansk, and the Moscow area. On the western leg of SAC's *Chrome Dome* routes, Siberia, and the Kamchatka and Vladivostok areas were target rich. Over 11,000 interceptors awaited bombers at medium and low altitudes, but *Chrome Dome* flights were safe from them if they stayed outside Soviet airspace. Western analysts certainly underestimated the effectiveness of Soviet radars, which were unexpectedly able to detect most U-2 overflights and later SR-71 Blackbird operations, curtailing overflights in Soviet airspace much sooner than the Pentagon anticipated.

Until the introduction of the SA-2 surface-to-air missile (SAM), Russia was also unable to counter the sporadic overflights of its territory by US and British reconnaissance aircraft, particularly the Lockheed U-2. To complain openly about them would have been an admission that Soviet air defenses were inadequate. Eisenhower's government was nervous about the flights, keeping them to a minimum despite the urgent need for information on Soviet strength. The shooting down of Gary Powers' U-2C, Article 360, on May 1, 1960 over Sverdlovsk while attempting to gather data on the Plesetsk ICBM base was therefore a

A mobile SAM system was needed in place of the Berkut to defend areas outside Moscow. Design of the S-75 (SA-2) Dvina began in 1953 with service entry occurring in 1957. In its S-75N Desna version with the high-frequency RSN-75 *Fan Song* radar, it ended U-2 spyplane flights over the Soviet Union in May 1960. (Dr Istvan Toperczer)

OPPOSITE B-47 LOW-ALTITUDE BOMBING SYSTEM (LABS) ATTACK

B-47s were SAC's principal bomber until 1959 when B-52s began to replace them. Phase-out occurred from 1963 to 1966, but one-third of the force was on ground alert during the 1962 Cuban Missile Crisis when LABS tactics would have been used. Reconnaissance versions remained in service throughout the *Chrome Dome* period, providing vital support.

major propaganda coup for Khrushchev. Eisenhower was obliged to take full responsibility for the disaster and the Soviet Union's consequent abandonment of talks on nuclear tests.

However, it had taken a number of SA-2s to achieve the shoot-down, as Soviet radar tracked the U-2. Numerous MiG and Sukhoi interceptors were alerted too late to try and catch it and then they failed to reach its 70,500ft altitude. The Chelyabinsk SA-2 regiment's launcher sustained a *Fan Song* electronic failure, while the missile batteries at Tyuratam were alerted too late to power up their radar sets. Finally, the radars of the PVO Air Defense regiment near Sverdlovsk picked up the U-2 and Maj Voronov ordered three SA-2s to be fired. Only one fired successfully, but it detonated near the U-2 destabilizing it and precipitating disintegration.

In all respects the PVO response was badly coordinated and it suggested that a number of B-52s, even at high altitude, might be able to evade a Soviet defense system that seemed unable to cover more than a few urban and high-value sites in the Soviet bloc's massive area. The experience of B-52 crews against the same missiles over North Vietnam showed that massive salvos of SA-2s from sites concentrated around a limited area were hard to avoid. It also showed that repeatedly using the same ingress and egress routes and tactics made the missile batteries' jobs much easier.

At high altitudes, bombers would have faced over a thousand SAM sites, many surrounding strategic targets. SA-2 Guideline SAMS could reach over 80,000ft, while the SA-3 Goa was effective at all altitudes. Much of the supervision of nuclear weapons was entrusted to the KGB and warheads were stored at some distance from bomber and missile bases.

Khrushchev adhered to the later Soviet diplomatic rule of avoiding outright nuclear war. Soviet planners believed that an all-out SAC assault was unlikely and that both sides would only commit a small proportion of their arsenals to an initial attack, given that there would be appalling destruction even then. However, Khrushchev took every opportunity to exaggerate

Until May 1, 1960, flights by CIA U-2s provided target information for potential SAC bomber and missile strikes. Thereafter, the information had to come mainly from satellite surveillance. (USAF)

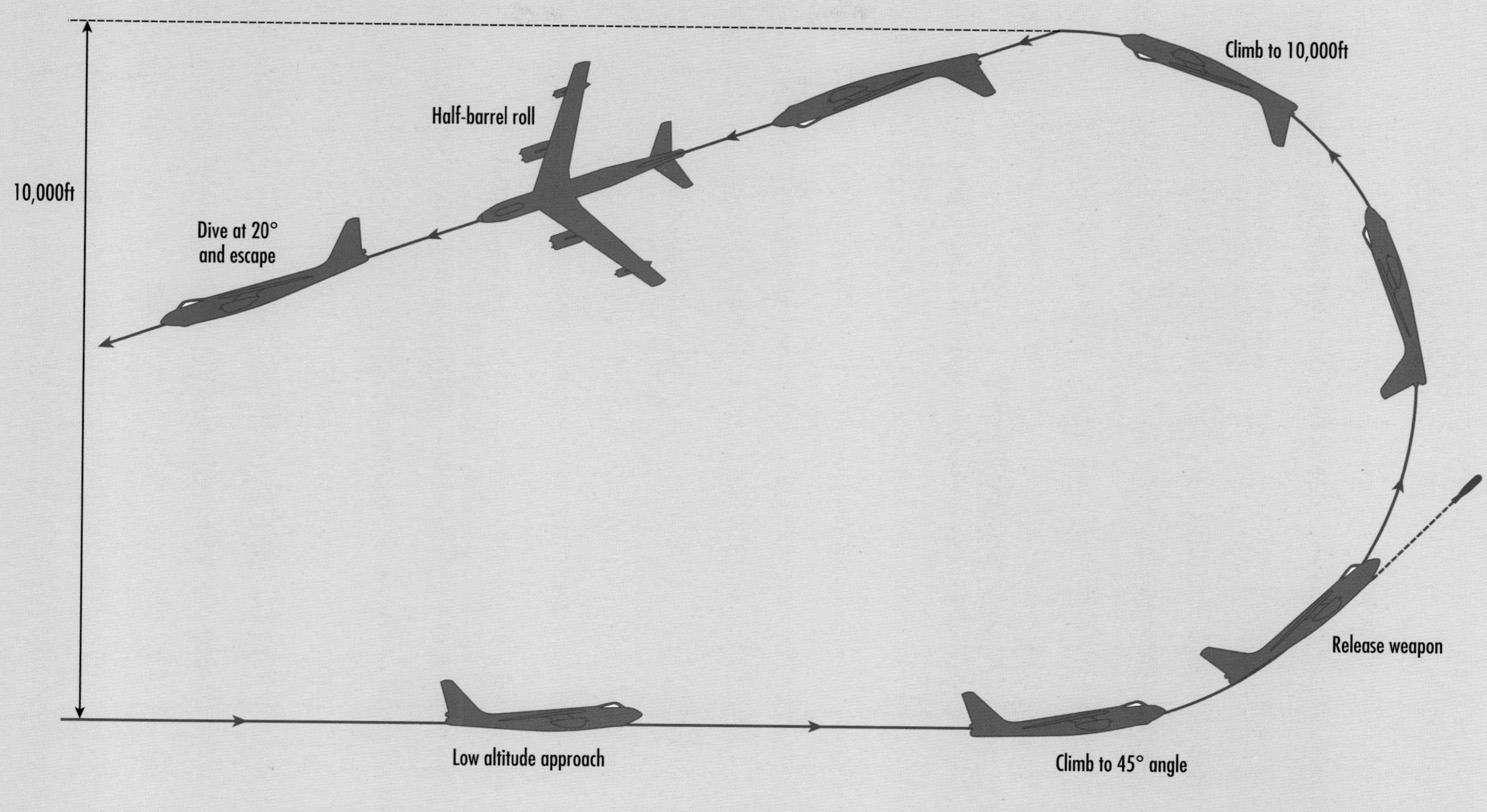
B-47 Low Altitude Bombing System (LABS) attack
10,000ft
Half-barrel roll
Climb to 10,000ft
Dive at 20°
and escape
Release weapon
Low altitude approach
Climb to 45° angle

RSN(A)-75 mobile radar units guided SA-2 missiles and they would have been targets for Hound Dog missiles wherever their locations could be ascertained. (Dr Istvan Toperczer)

his military strength and inflame Western anxieties. In potential stand-offs with the West, such as the 1958 Berlin Crisis and Soviet support for China's threat to occupy islands off Nationalist Taiwan, he showed that he would gamble on the opposition backing down if he used belligerent bluffing tactics, forcing disputes to the brink of war. Meanwhile, his more surreptitious nuclear plans included the placement of nuclear mines in many US harbors, secretly off-loaded from "harmless" merchant vessels.

Soviet military hardware designers sought to keep up with the perceived threats from the West and with Soviet expansionist aspirations. MiG-15 fighters scored heavily against SAC's B-29 force in Korea and when the SAC Tactics group pitted a B-47 against a MiG-15 flown by top USAF ace pilots the expertly flown bomber was unable to lose the MiG in a series of engagements. In similar tests flown later with a B-52 under attack by a MiG-17, it was clear that the bomber could usually out-maneuver the MiG at high altitudes. At 40,000ft a 45-degree turn with the speed brakes extended was enough to make the small-winged fighters that tail-chased B-52s in practice interceptions overshoot and fall away. The B-52 was also far better equipped with countermeasures than the B-47 to deal with ground defenses. When US bombers were forced to adopt low-altitude tactics by the expansion of Soviet SAM networks, the interceptor fighter regained prominence and a new generation of fighters and air-to-air missiles was produced, starting with the supersonic MiG-21, which was designed to catch B-52s at any altitude.

The steady improvement in Soviet defenses forced SAC to abandon its reliance on high-altitude bombing strategies. From 1959 onwards, low-altitude, radar-avoiding approaches were required, causing increased fuel consumption and reduction of range. SAC had to establish seven low-level "Oil Burner" training routes in the USA, each one 500 miles long and 20 miles wide with simulated targets en route and inevitable environmental consequences. However, on the rare occasions that the defenses were tested by accidental or even by deliberate overflights of Soviet territory, the results were surprisingly poor. This situation continued beyond the 1960s with two Korean airliners being misidentified as US military aircraft or undetected for many miles into Soviet airspace and a Cessna 172 flying undetected from Finland to Red Square, Moscow in 1987.

While Soviet military technology often matched that of the West, the efficiency of its armed forces has always been compromised by the wide gulf between the status of aircrew officers, who traditionally came from better-educated or more socially advantaged backgrounds, and the conscripts who were tasked with maintaining the aircraft. Officers had less demanding training than their US counterparts and were eligible for many privileges and promotion at very young ages. Defecting MiG-25 interceptor pilot Lt Victor Belenko told US interrogators in 1976 that his unit flew very little and drank a lot. The most promising recruits were directed to the Strategic Rocket Force with the next level of talent going to the bomber units. Conscripts, all eligible for two years' service at 18 years old, were paid far less and often treated inhumanely. Low motivation, poor education, alcohol abuse, corruption, and prolonged separation from their families were common, with obvious consequences for their combat efficiency. All units were under constant surveillance by the KGB and *Zampolit* political agents for signs of political non-conformity or disloyalty. The five branches of the Soviet services required an annual intake of over 1.5 million recruits, reliant upon forcible conscription. B-52 pilots could draw some comfort from the Soviet reliance on numbers of personnel rather than efficient teamwork and leadership.

While the West considerably overestimated the Soviet threat in the 1950s, it tended to misjudge the build-up of new ICBMs in the mid-1960s for the Soviet Strategic Rocket Force. Instead of trying to match America's huge bomber fleet, the Soviet Triad focussed on missiles such as the SS-9, which was larger and far more devastating than the standard US Minuteman, albeit less reliable and less sophisticated. They also began to match US missile strength numerically. By April 1961, there were also 2,471 nuclear bombs in the Soviet armory. Soviet planners considered the strategy of launching all their ICBMs as soon as a US missile attack was detected so that they would, in effect, cross in the air. It was concluded that there would be insufficient time to make the required decision to do so.

The Soviet Union also developed the world's most formidable nuclear weapon. Its 1961 AN602 60,000lb *Tsar Bomba* hydrogen bomb yielded 58 megatons and could have been modified to 100 megatons, but there was concern that this might trigger a massive atmospheric "burn" covering whole continents. Dropped from a Tu-95V bomber over the Novaya Zemlya island test range, its detonation fireball could be seen over 600 miles away and the shock broke windows 480 miles distant. *Tsar Bomba* was ten times as powerful as the total of explosives dropped during World War II and over 1,500 times more destructive than the US *Little Boy* that was dropped on Hiroshima. Fortunately, its development was ended with the signing of the 1963 Nuclear Test Ban Treaty, which prohibited nuclear tests in the atmosphere and outer space. However, the propaganda effects of *Tsar Bomba* lived on. Its origins may have been based on the knowledge of SAC's brief demands in the late 1950s for a 60-megaton weapon.

Supersonic MiG-19s could have provided serious opposition to B-52s at any altitudes, as would the MiG-21, which was designed specifically to oppose US bombers and spyplanes. (Wiki/Rosa06)

B-52C-040-BO 53-0400 had a long service life beginning with the 42nd BW at Loring AFB, Maine in June 1956 and ending in September 1971 when most early B-52s were withdrawn and stored. It was among the variants destroyed within the 1991 SALT agreement. Thermal-reflecting white undersides and larger external fuel tanks were introduced with the B-52C variant. (USAF)

Overall, however, Soviet missile capability still lagged behind America's, one reason why visits by inspectors to monitor an arms limitation treaty were refused. Khrushchev was aware that his ICBMs could only be used for a first strike as their R-16 rockets took hours to prepare for launch, unlike SAC's Minuteman. His silos, bombers, and stockpile of over 3,300 nuclear weapons would therefore have been attacked by *Chrome Dome* B-52s or missiles before he could mount any sort of retaliation to an American first strike.

Cuba

The Cuban Missile Crisis in October 1962 demonstrated Khrushchev's willingness to go beyond a conventional defensive stance and provoke his potential enemy. It also justified LeMay's pro-bomber campaigning, SAC's integrated reconnaissance capability, and Kennedy's flexible response doctrine, in which the reaction to a threat could involve conventional weapons rather than an all-out nuclear attack. Khrushchev had interpreted the disastrous CIA-sponsored Bay of Pigs invasion of Cuba as proof of weakness by President Kennedy. He decided to test American resolve by using Cuba as a base for missiles that could strike SAC bases quickly before they could get bombers airborne. He also wanted the Jupiter missiles that America had placed in Turkey to be moved out of range of the Soviet Union.

The United States was fortunate to have some access to the truth about Soviet military power and political intentions until 1962 via Col Oleg Penkovsky, who supplied information revealing the major weaknesses in Soviet nuclear and conventional defenses. This encouraged President Kennedy to take a firm stand after the discovery of Soviet antiaircraft missiles on Cuban territory. Cuba's leader, Fidel Castro, meanwhile promised to make New York "another Hiroshima" if he was attacked. Kennedy risked Khrushchev's potential isolation of West Berlin if seriously challenged. Reconnaissance revealed offensive missiles including 42 SS-4/R-12 *Sandal* medium-range missiles and their warheads together with 36 2K6 *Luna/Frog-3* short-range missiles, 12 with nuclear warheads and four targeted on the US

Guatanamo base on the island. Fears of a devastating surprise attack similar to Pearl Harbor were revived again.

Kennedy was aware of the dire consequences of even one missile hitting a US city, so he was therefore prepared to make an executive decision to trade the obsolescent Turkish-based missiles for Khrushchev's, which were returned to the USSR from October 28. Khrushchev's own missile force was not yet fully operational, but 132 ICBMs were available by October 22.

For the USA, in the absence of flexible response and the alert bomber force (*see Attacker's Capabilities*), a full-scale ICBM response would have been the only alternative to accepting the Soviet fortification of Cuba. The proximity to the USA of nuclear missiles would have severely reduced America's advantage in deliverable nuclear warheads, amounting to around 5,000 against the Soviet Union's 300 at the time, as many would probably have reached their targets from Cuba. Gen Walter Sweeney, in charge of Tactical Air Command (TAC), admitted that even 500 sorties with conventional weapons would not ensure the destruction of all the Soviet missiles.

Kennedy was therefore persuaded that a blockade of Soviet supply ships bringing longer-range missiles was preferable to direct strikes, though US generals including LeMay (who Kennedy found infuriating) wanted stronger reactions. Kennedy reflected that he had confidence in the final outcome of US diplomacy, commenting that, because of the recently activated Minuteman force, "Mr Khrushchev knew that we had an ace in the hole with our improved strategic forces." Generally, US nuclear superiority over the Soviet Union's in 1962 was decisive, but short-lived.

Sino-Soviet missiles

US intelligence did become aware of Soviet attempts to match its effective SAM defenses against bombers with an antiballistic missile (ABM) network, beginning with the "Galosh" system around Moscow. This system was ineffective, but it did prompt fears that US bombers and missiles might now be unable to reach their targets. The development of a US ABM

B-52Cs and a single B-52D lined up at Westover AFB, Massachusetts early in 1957. The three 99th BW squadrons operated a mixture of B-52Cs and B-52Ds as well as a few B-52Bs. The nearest aircraft has had its radome removed for maintenance of its MA-6A bombing/navigation system. (USAF)

system was investigated, culminating in President Ronald Reagan's vastly expensive Star Wars ABM proposals.

It was also suggested that Soviet ABMs could be defeated by using multiple warheads in each missile (or an air-launched cruise missile). Multiple independently targeted re-entry vehicles (MIRV) could be targeted on both missile silos and ABM defenses, using one carrier missile for a first strike. Targets that were still active could then be re-attacked, preferably with the new strategic bomber that SAC was demanding in 1967. McNamara, who had previously resisted the idea of nuclear attacks on cities, also conceded that this second wave of bombers or missiles could be used to devastate large population centers. *Chrome Dome* (airborne alert) B-52s would have been best placed for those follow-up attacks.

China's acquisition of thermonuclear weapons alarmed the USSR and the USA equally and made the ABM proposals more attractive to both governments, but their mutual anxieties about spiralling defense costs eventually led to the Strategic Arms Limitation Talks (SALT) in 1972.

From the mid-1960s the Soviet Union's defense strategy included a planned response to nuclear attack, updated twice annually. All silo-based ICBMs would have been launched at airfields, ports, and major infrastructure targets rather than the USA's 1,000 missile silos, which would theoretically already have expended their contents. Like the USA, however, the main reliance was on the deterrent effect of such a potential onslaught. Its most potent weapon, however, was its fleet of Project 667 Yankee nuclear submarines armed with R-27 Zyb (SS-N-6 Serb) nuclear missiles. Patrolling off the US coast, they could launch salvoes of missiles from 164ft below the surface. With a range of at least 1,500 miles and a flight-time of around 13 minutes, they put all SAC facilities in jeopardy.

Although the Soviet bomber fleet was eventually provided with limited in-flight refueling, its primary focus was on European, Chinese, and antishipping operations rather than strategic attacks on North America. Khrushchev was no doubt also aware that the United States kept a very large number of tactical nuclear weapons in Europe that would have to be eliminated before any attempt at invasion.

Improved Soviet defenses made low-level approaches to the target inevitable, although not in close formation cells, as seen in this firepower demonstration by B-52Fs. (USAF)

THE CREWS

Training

SAC's two main Cold War bombers began service within a few years of each other. Boeing's B-47 entered SAC's war plan in June 1953, almost six years after its first flight. Problems remained and the first 400 aircraft arrived with inactivated ejection seats due to safety deficiencies. Crews had to tolerate that situation until the mid-1950s. The aircraft's central K-2 bombing system, originating in 1944, relied on 370 vacuum tubes in 41 components totaling 20,000 parts. Checking out the system took eight hours. The initial aircraft were deficient in range until LeMay had them fitted with in-flight refueling capability and external fuel tanks.

B-52B Stratofortress deliveries began in June 1955 to the 93rd BW at Castle AFB, California, where most B-52Bs were eventually based and the 4017th CCTS began training crews there. Many early crews transitioned from B-47s or B-36s. Castle continued as the sole base for all B-52 flying training despite its susceptibility to fog. Two more SAC wings, the 42nd BW at Loring AFB, Maine and the 99th BW at Westover AFB, Massachusetts received B-52Cs in 1956. Pilot and co-pilot training worked on a three-day cycle: mission planning, flying a ten-hour mission, and a third day devoted to debriefing. Night missions took off at 2200hrs, returning at 0800hrs the next day. For *Chrome Dome* a third pilot was essential to cover rest periods for the other pilots. He sat in the instructor pilot's seat, which did not eject, behind the other pilots.

One of LeMay's first priorities was to train enough aircrew as navigator/bombardiers for the new bomber. Radar bombardiers and EWs all had to qualify as navigators before cross-training in their advanced specialism. From 1960, all the relevant training took place at Mather AFB, California until 1992. Until 1960, most B-52 aircrew had World War II training, but they were retiring by the late 1960s and their younger replacements often came from college cadet detachments via Reserve Officers Training Corps (ROTC).

Bombardiers for B-52C/D models studied the AN/ASQ-48 bombing/navigation system using the APS-108 radar, while those assigned to later models learned the AN/ASQ-38. Their work was based on close monitoring of a complex and initially confusing radar display. The Convair T-29C/D "Flying Classroom" was used for all navigation/ bombardier training.

The 92nd BW crew of B-52D-070-BO 56-0590 head for the small entry hatch at the double for a practice alert at Fairchild AFB, Washington State in 1961. Airborne alert crews knew that, in the event of war, they might escape a nuclear attack by being on patrol, but they would probably return to find that their base and families had been turned to dust. Few of them thought that they would ever be ordered to deliver their weapons rather than maintain a forceful deterrent posture. (USAF)

Like the B-52, it had a 6in. radar control tracking handle in the radar navigator's position, which enabled him to use weapon-aiming crosshairs on his screen during the bombing run. The screen also showed wind speed, aircraft heading, and information for the pilot to make a blind landing, among other functions. These systems kept track of the bomber's position, sending the autopilot heading corrections for automatic navigation to a target or other fixed, radar-reflective initial point (IP) and determining the moment of bomb release. Additional information on ground speed and drift angle came from the APN-108 Doppler radar.

Training focussed on the main nuclear weapons delivery procedure, or Radar Synchronous Bomb Run. As the T-29D approached its target, simulating a nuclear attack, the navigator/bombardier placed his crosshairs on the aiming point and the system's computers calculated the bomb release line (BRL), taking into account weapon characteristics, winds, altitude, and airspeed. On the flight deck the pilot monitored heading data on his pilot's deflection indicator (PDI), correcting where necessary to keep the line central. The bomb release point was indicated when a "to go" meter showed a zero.

Radar bombing system (RBS) scores were the main measure for evaluating crew performance. Some RBS targets were located on trains, the RBS Express system, running within low-level training routes in three areas to complicate the radar-bombardiers' tasks. The chosen routes were similar to those on approaches to potential Soviet targets, offering bird strikes, stray private aircraft, sudden weather changes, and irregular terrain as additional hazards. The effort of low-level flight in turbulent air demanded the pilot's full strength to wrestle with the control yoke, while the co-pilot operated the throttles to maintain the right speed. That task was exacerbated by constant vibration making the multiple gauges hard to read.

Former radar navigator Capt Robert Newton recalled those bombing procedures. "We used the [ASQ-38] radar bombing system to drop one, or multiple drops on high or low targets. There were several cities and towns designated with several targets. Everything was scored by Radar Bomb Scoring sites tracking us in and we turned on a radio tone. When the tone stopped a needle lifted off a chart and we called down several pieces of information so that they could score in feet and direction how close we came." He described RBS missions as "hours of boredom interspersed with moments of panic. The typical practice mission lasted ten to twelve hours. It was called a Profile Mission because we did everything in the same order as if it was a real war mission. When flying at low level we flew at about 280kts and stayed straight and level at about 500ft

The pilot (left) and co-pilot of RB-52B-005-BO 52-0005 maintain almost full power on all eight throttles after take-off. The "Boeing B-52" center boss on the control yoke became a much-coveted souvenir. (Boeing)

Wichita-built B-52E-050-BW 57-0096 stands connected and ready for a *Chrome Dome* with Hound Dogs aboard. It flew with five bomb wings throughout the Cold War at a time when, expressing the strange logic of nuclear deterrence, Secretary of Defense McNamara stated that the USA and the USSR should both possess "the capability of surviving a first strike and retaliating selectively," providing "a more stable balance of terror." (All McNamara)

altitude until we made our bomb runs. Occasionally we would make high-speed runs at 325kts and it became a real wild ride." With the addition of terrain avoidance radar, one of the Project *Big Four* updates, "we humped and dumped over the hills and mountains, and it became a real rollercoaster ride." The B-52's 185ft wingspan ruled out all but shallow turns at those altitudes.

Training in the 1960s included low-altitude navigation sorties along the 500-mile long Oil Burner routes (inspired by the aircraft's black smoke trails) over thinly populated areas of the western USA, flying at 450mph as low as 200ft above ground level or even within the Grand Canyon. The installation of terrain avoidance radar in later B-52s enabled this to happen at night. Excessive turbulence, particularly near mountainous terrain or from clear air turbulence, put enormous strains on the big B-52s' airframes and 13 were lost in 11 years due to structural failure. Several involved the 48ft vertical stabilizers breaking off the tall-tail B-52B to B-52F models. Pilot John Paul Marsh and four crewmen died in a January 1961 crash near Monticello when a horizontal gust removed the tail of their B-52 over mountainous Utah terrain. In 1963 a second, together with seven crew suffered a similar fate over mountains in Greenville, Maine. Days later a third lost its tail over New Mexico's Sangre de Cristo mountains. Investigators found that in each case the tail had been torn

Suggesting the caption "Where shall we go today?" this group of 525th BS, 4136th SW crew dogs pose on Minot AFB, North Dakota's concrete in 1961. In the background is their B-52H-150-BW 60-0040, lost with the 410th BW in December 1988 when an explosion occurred after a landing overshoot at K I Sawyer AFB, Michigan. (USAF)

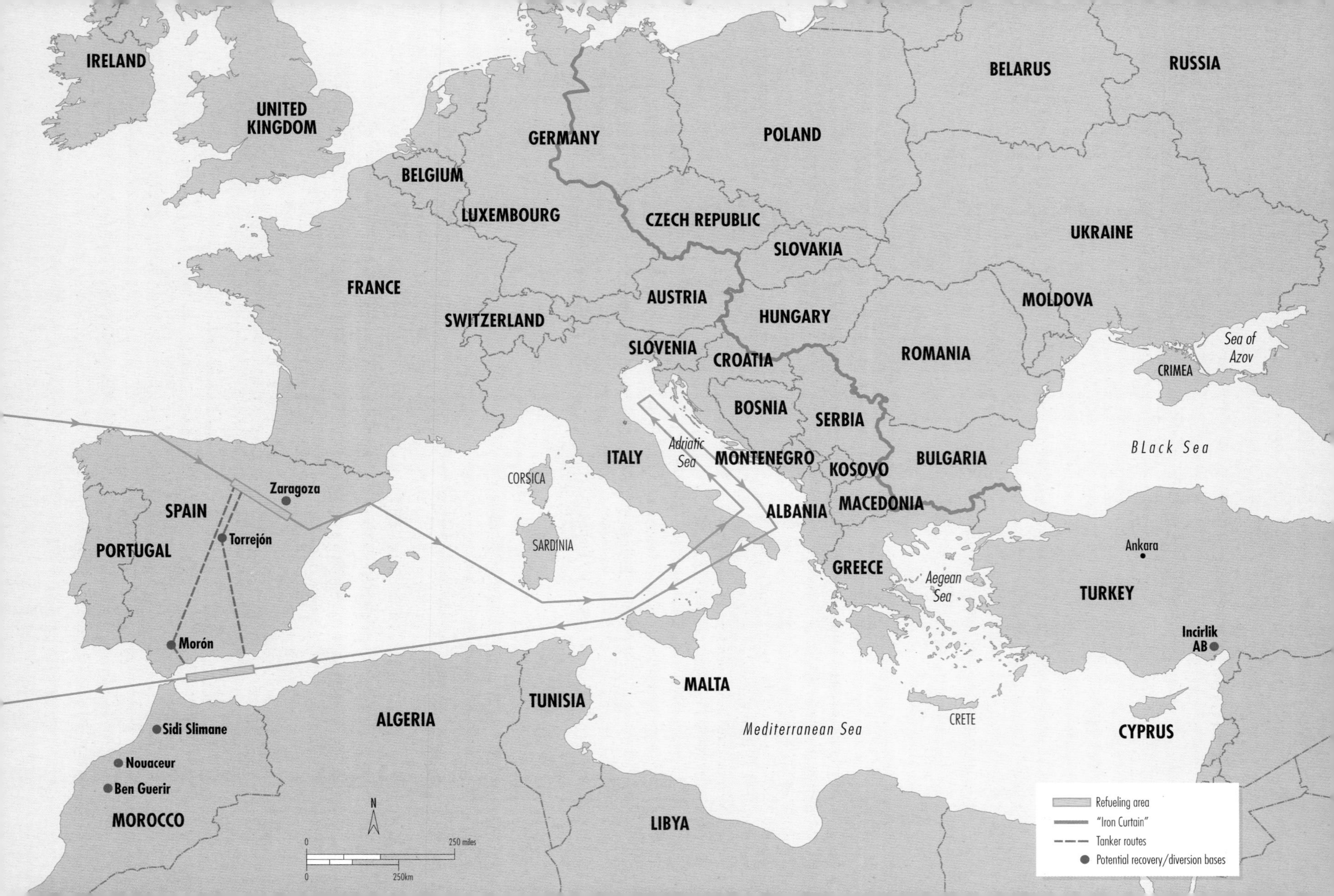
IRELAND
UNITED KINGDOM
GERMANY
POLAND
BELARUS
RUSSIA
BELGIUM
LUXEMBOURG
CZECH REPUBLIC
UKRAINE
SLOVAKIA
FRANCE
AUSTRIA
HUNGARY
MOLDOVA
SWITZERLAND
SLOVENIA
CROATIA
ROMANIA
Sea of Azov
CRIMEA
BOSNIA
SERBIA
Black Sea
ITALY
Adriatic Sea
MONTENEGRO
KOSOVO
BULGARIA
CORSICA
Zaragoza
SPAIN
ALBANIA
MACEDONIA
Torrejón
PORTUGAL
SARDINIA
Ankara
GREECE
Aegean Sea
TURKEY
Morón
Incirlik AB
MALTA
TUNISIA
ALGERIA
Sidi Slimane
Mediterranean Sea
CRETE
CYPRUS
Nouaceur
Ben Guerir
MOROCCO
LIBYA
N
0
250 miles
250km
Refueling area
"Iron Curtain"
Tanker routes
Potential recovery/diversion bases

OPPOSITE SOUTHERN *CHROME DOME* ROUTE

away from the cracked and fatigued horseshoe-shaped Bulkhead 1655 in the rear fuselage and extensive reinforcement was needed to remedy an "acute" situation. Repairs were made during phase maintenance, but the fleet was not grounded, and the losses were apparently regarded as sustainable during a Cold War situation.

SAC training exercises became a national concern at times. For a *Sky Shield II* event in 1961 from Carswell AFB all civilian and commercial air traffic was closed down for 24 hours while a force of up to 500 bombers including B-52s flew over the northeastern United States and Canada, posing as incoming Soviet bombers entering over Hudson Bay to test Air Defense Command interceptors. They succeeded in penetrating the defenses in around 95 percent of the sorties, boosting SAC's confidence in its chances against Soviet defenses.

SAC rules

To provide reassurance that the nuclear mission was in the hands of exceptionally responsible and well-motivated aircrew, SAC initiated a Human Reliability Program which focussed on a crew member's performance, behavior, reputation, and private life and ensured that no individual could be alone near a nuclear weapon or in sole charge of arming one. Background checks by the USAF's investigative branch and the FBI ensured that any risky behavioral anomalies were detected before personnel received their Top Secret security rating. Thereafter, strict conformity to SAC rules was required and frequently monitored. Trainees entered the nuclear weapons phase of their courses at Mather AFB's Special Weapons School, where they learned the power and effects of bombs such as the commonly used Mk 28, 55 times as destructive as the bomb dropped on Hiroshima (which itself had the equivalent force of 3,000 conventional bombers' payloads) or the far more powerful 25-megaton Mk 41. The 9,000lb B53 was also carried on *Chrome Dome* flights.

On operational bases, nuclear weapons, guarded by police in jeeps fitted with .50 machine guns, were loaded into bombers behind black curtains within an area cordoned off with red

The tail gunner in B-52s prior to the B-52G had an unenviable task, occupying a small, isolated cabin 150ft to the rear. There, as former gunner Capt Danny Burnett recalled, he was subjected to turbulent air causing the "Boeing Bounce." "The tail moved three feet for every foot the nose moved and it was considered a sign of macho to have had a helmet cracked on your head from the ride." The radar warning "horns" project each side of this B-52D's back-up periscope gunsight. (USAF)

rope. In the B-36 and B-47 eras, all personnel involved in the process including maintainers carried side-arms for additional security. Anyone crossing the red or yellow barrier markings of this "No Lone Zone" and approaching the aircraft alone without appropriate clearance would quickly find themselves spread-eagled on the ground with an M16 carbine pointed at a vital organ. Access to a nuclear storage area, with its 17ft thick concrete walls, required FBI "Q" clearance. A changeover of alert crews at a B-52 had to be managed exactly so that the departing crew handed over control of the weapons and pre-flight routines before the outgoing crew left. The double-locked "secrets box," containing the EWO code book and color-coded mission execution slips, was already in the aircraft and locked down by armed guards. Any discrepancy in this procedure triggered the arrival of a *Helping Hand* security squad to interrogate the unfortunate crew members. An incoming crew would also bring a weapons box containing six .38 calibre guns for token personal protection in the event of a shoot-down in hostile territory, or as sometimes claimed, to neutralize any crew member who had a "Dr Strangelove moment" and tried to drop a bomb.

Inspection of the nuclear weapons in the bomb-bay included checking the barometric settings for the detonation altitude required for each target. The bomb's ball-shaped core contained the "urchin" sphere of fissionable plutonium material that initiated nuclear fission with the uranium shell that surrounded it. An outer lens arrangement of up to 5,000lb of high explosive detonated and forced them together. The core was inserted into the bomb during the flight, usually by the radar navigator who was part of the three-man team – co-pilot, aircraft commander, and radar bombardier/navigator – who were trained to handle special weapons in the B-36 and B-47 era. From 1959, thermonuclear devices, known as sealed-pit weapons, required no on-board preparation, since the core was already sealed inside the weapon. Weapons were distributed from the Los Alamitos National Laboratory, New Mexico to National Stockpile Sites on bases in the USA and on 24 locations abroad in a system codenamed *Water Supply*.

SAC's state of Cold War readiness was measured in a series of Defense Readiness Condition (DEFCON) states and the Emergency War Order (EWO), both under the management of the National Command Authority, the US president, and his secretary of defense. Control of bombers, tankers, command posts, reconnaissance aircraft, and long-range missiles came under their auspices within the closely guarded SIOP. Within the plan, a gradation of "key hours" was introduced, starting with H-Hour as the trigger for all operations. At A-Hour forces would begin to raise their alert level and the RB-47H force was launched to collect electronic intelligence over Europe and the Far East. E-Hour signified that the SIOP strike force had been "executed," with the launch of the alert strike force happening at L-Hour.

B-52B La Fortaleza is connected to an air conditioning unit. Bases like Biggs AFB, Texas could become intolerably hot. For a ground crew, day-to-day maintenance levels ran from Code 1 status (fuel, water, and oil replenishment only) to Code 3 (flight safety-related problems that required the plane to be removed from the flying schedule), with any issues recorded on the aircraft's Form 781. (USAF)

DEFCON states began at DEFCON-5 (normal peacetime conditions), through DEFCON-4 (SAC's usual Cold War posture, including "enhanced intelligence activities"), and DEFCON-3 (a response to increased international tensions over, for example, the Yom Kippur War in 1973) at which security was increased, aircraft were dispersed to other civilian and Air Guard bases, and airborne command and control aircraft were launched. At DEFCON-2 all SAC forces were put on high alert via Emergency Action Messages (EAMs), personnel were called back from leave, and alert crews who would man the first wave of attacks were restricted to base and issued with Combat Mission Folders to enable briefings to be organized. Other flights apart from

Of the 14 cases of structural failure in B-52s caused by turbulent air, there was one extraordinary survivor on January 10, 1964. Boeing test pilot Chuck Fisher managed to bring an armed B-52H home after losing its vertical stabilizer in turbulence around the Colorado Rocky Mountains. With marginal control, he and co-pilot Dick Curry managed to land 61-0023 (on loan from the 19th BW) at Blytheville AFB, Arkansas. (USAF)

airborne alerts were canceled. For the final stage, DEFCON-1 crews were told to prepare their aircraft for launch and keep them in a "cocked" situation for as long as necessary. Another reserve *Giant Lance* force took off and moved to a patrol station from which they would make any necessary follow-up attacks after the first wave had executed theirs.

EWO Index (Red Dot) messages, written in a Sealed Authenticator System code, were issued to SAC crews by senior commanders over the base command radio frequency to launch strike forces when a conflict was considered imminent. From March 1960, the *Short Order* sideband high-frequency communications system used four stations at USAF headquarters throughout the USA. It provided "positive control" over SAC bombers as they flew towards their targets. When they reached the "fail-safe" point (later renamed "Positive Control" point) in the mission profile, just outside enemy airspace, they would turn back unless they received an encrypted message to proceed. Aircraft commanders were given plastic envelopes with a code word printed on them. If they received a message containing the same code, they opened the envelope and found another code word, which had to be authenticated via a message from a ground station. The message had to be translated using a code book from a double-locked box and agreed by the EW, navigator, and radar-navigator. It instructed them to proceed to the "H-Hour Control Line," an imaginary line around Soviet territory and outside the range of early warning radars. H-Hour signified the start point for all operations, preceded by A-Hour at which point forces for an attack were generated and E-Hour for "Execution time of the SIOP strike force."

B-52D-20-BW 55-0675 from the 28th BW visits RAF Fairford, UK in April 1964. B-52 deployments to Fairford were still regular half a century later. (Terry Panopalis collection)

When the initial Alpha force (alert) bombers proceeded to their "last chance" Positive Control Turn-around Points on receipt of a short Red Dot 1, they were followed by the second (Charlie) wave, launched by a Red Dot 2 message. A (Foxtrot) force of reserve bombers and tankers would take off on receipt of Red Dot 3 for a retaliatory mission. A final "go code" Red Dot 4 Emergency Action Message enabled bombers to continue to their targets at high altitude, then to a pre-planned Start Descent Point to a low altitude and a Terrain Avoidance Point to evade enemy interceptors. Some of the flight would be over poorly mapped territory with unknown terrain obstacles for ground-hugging bombers.

Targets could have included all major Soviet cities as one SIOP option, or its nuclear bases as another pre-emptive possibility, where nuclear strikes would be conducted. Later options included selected strikes on the Soviet leadership and command centers.

Before 1970, Red Dot communications could be preceded or replaced by Blue Dot messages to establish DEFCON levels or changes, command arrangements, and "reaction posture," which would probably mean preparing the aircraft, starting the engines, and then shutting down, although the aircraft and crew remained in place for further orders.

Shortly before the 1962 Cuban Missile Crisis, President Kennedy altered the structure of the command system for nuclear forces, creating the National Military Command System to give the president greater control of the intelligence and warning processes and military responses involved in nuclear operations. Permissive Action Links (PALs), electronic locks on each weapon, which required digital codes to enable arming and detonation, were introduced for weapons located in Europe. All nuclear weapons were subject to the "two-man rule" after mid-1962. Each action involved in handling or preparing a weapon had to be carried out by pairs of qualified operators. They had access to a safe containing the PAL codes, which had to be entered separately by each person, causing another eight-digit set of codes to be transmitted before the weapon could be armed after two keys, each at different locations, were turned by the team simultaneously. Aboard a B-52 the process had to be authenticated by three crew members, as did the process of arming a weapon. For nuclear missiles two parallel pairs of crewmen were needed for additional safety.

Pulling alert

When the Soviet Union acquired long-range ballistic missiles in 1957 it became clear that operating SAC assets from a few large bases offered the Soviet Union easier targets, although bases in central USA such as Minot AFB, North Dakota or Ellsworth, South Dakota were less vulnerable to submarine-launched missiles. A policy of dispersal was initiated in 1957 in which the existing large bomber wings of 45 B-52s and around 20 tankers were split into three 15-aircraft units, two squadrons being allocated to other bases effectively as separate bomb wings with ten to 15 tankers each. A wing had 135 crewmen, allowing one and a half six-man crews to each B-52. Twenty-two bases were used in all, including basic facilities such as Amarillo AFB and Sheppard AFB in Texas, dispersal fields for the 7th BW at Carswell AFB. Half the aircraft at each base were kept on ground alert. Tests in 1961 proved that these aircraft could be launched at the overall rate of 200 per minute.

The ground alert program was also modified in 1958 so that 11 SAC wings, one-third of the force, were on alert status at any time. It was also recognized that the alert pattern fell into four phases: ground alert, flight planning, flying sorties, and a rest day. A fourth squadron was therefore added to each wing to follow this pattern more easily on a squadron rota basis. In addition, maintenance was centralized for each wing via organizational maintenance squadrons (OMS). Some air divisions and wings which controlled ICBM units as well as bombers were renamed strategic wings and 14 had been established by the end of 1958. In 1961, they were renamed strategic aerospace wings and briefly given four-figure designations until 1963. By March 1964, the number of alert bombers was slightly less than the total

B-52G-105-BW 58-0231 of the 97th BW at Blytheville AFB, Arkansas with a GAM-72A Quail awaiting loading into its bomb-bay. This aircraft flew from Blytheville from February 1960 until June 1963 when it was re-assigned to the 416th BW at Griffiss AFB, New York state. (USAF)

of ICBMs on alert, a continuing trend. Bomb wings were usually allocated *Chrome Dome* airborne alert routes according to the geographical location of their bases. The 768th BW at Larson AFB, Washington State, for example, usually took their B-52Ds on the northern routes to the Arctic region. However, B-52Ds from further south at Sheppard AFB, Texas would head to Thule AFB or the Mediterranean.

As SAC's force expanded, its burden of responsibility in handling nuclear weapons became increasingly demanding. Extraordinary levels of security and monitoring had to accompany all its activities, giving rise to many apocryphal stories. In one, a pilot's wife was enjoying a noisy dance party at an SAC base and was overheard shouting to a friend that she should not worry about a potential war as her husband had Moscow as his designated target. This was overheard and immediately reported to the wing commander who shut down the dance and lectured the audience on security. He then called all aircrew and planners together and assigned different targets to each crew, leaving them to make the arduous, detailed study for their new missions for the rest of the night. Security was the priority in a situation where aircrew families were aware that a wartime mission would probably be a one-way flight and that their own home base was a primary target for Soviet missiles. Each base had its own evacuation plan. At the time that SAC reached its "50 percent alert" condition, 90 percent of "crewdogs" were married with children.

Each of the 40 operational B-52 squadrons available in the mid-1960s included roughly three crews for each of its usual 15 or 16 aircraft and a similar number for each tanker unit. In all, the total of combat-ready aircrew in SAC averaged almost 20,000 at that time. Crews, which received a group ID such a "Crew R-16" when they were Combat Ready, were carefully selected for compatibility on the assumption that they would fly together for several years. The risk of clashes between crew members during a long, hazardous *Chrome Dome* flight loaded with special weapons was intolerable. When a crew qualified in training as Combat Ready it was said to be "SACumcized," a term which was also applied to fighter pilots who were reluctantly reassigned to B-52s.

Further training was needed in the Positive Control procedures needed to handle nuclear weapons. These included a two-man policy when crew were around a loaded B-52, so that no crewman was left alone in the vicinity of nuclear devices. Perfection was the order, from performance during a mission to the color of his socks (regulation blue).

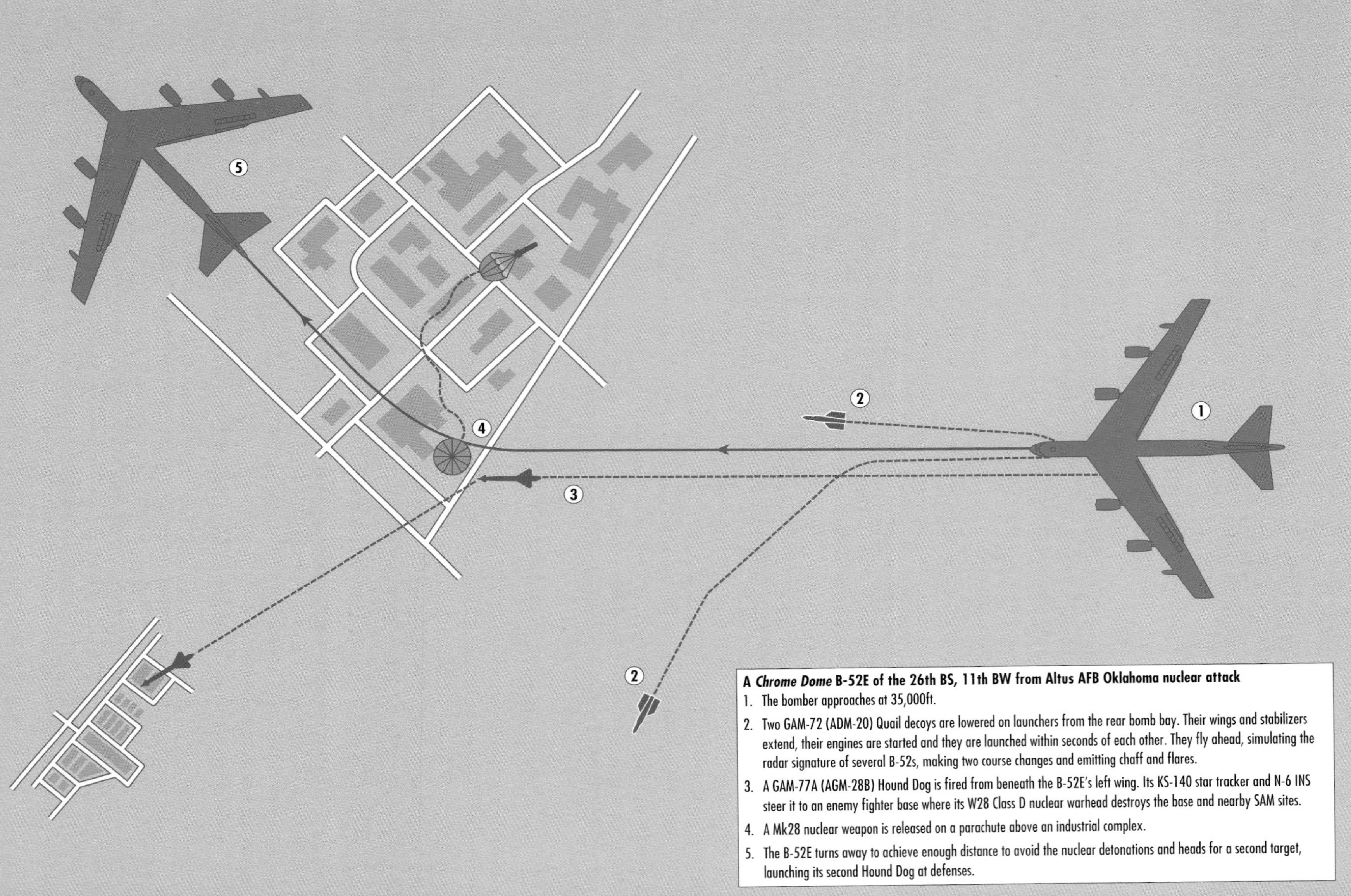

A *Chrome Dome* B-52E of the 26th BS, 11th BW from Altus AFB Oklahoma nuclear attack

1. The bomber approaches at 35,000ft.
2. Two GAM-72 (ADM-20) Quail decoys are lowered on launchers from the rear bomb bay. Their wings and stabilizers extend, their engines are started and they are launched within seconds of each other. They fly ahead, simulating the radar signature of several B-52s, making two course changes and emitting chaff and flares.
3. A GAM-77A (AGM-28B) Hound Dog is fired from beneath the B-52E's left wing. Its KS-140 star tracker and N-6 INS steer it to an enemy fighter base where its W28 Class D nuclear warhead destroys the base and nearby SAM sites.
4. A Mk28 nuclear weapon is released on a parachute above an industrial complex.
5. The B-52E turns away to achieve enough distance to avoid the nuclear detonations and heads for a second target, launching its second Hound Dog at defenses.

OPPOSITE B-52E NUCLEAR ATTACK ON AN ENEMY AIR BASE

The USAF's Operational Readiness Inspection (ORI) procedure was particularly draconian for SAC units. The first warning of a week-long inspection by the SAC Inspector General (IG) and a team of up to 60 came when their KC-135 was seen on final approach. The team quickly issued a simulated war order and checked in minute detail how a unit's alert crews responded. The rest of its bombers and tankers then had to be generated to full combat standard, with nuclear weapon uploaded. A full simulated wartime mission was then flown along internal US routes after the special weapons had been downloaded and evaluators installed in all the aircraft. A 75 percent faultless performance was the minimum requirement for the wing to pass, while annual written proficiency tests for flight crew needed a 100 percent score. Meanwhile, every aspect of the wing's operations from the motor pool to the dental clinic were being minutely inspected ready for the ORI critique at the week's end. Praise could be given, but even minor infringements of the rules could and did lead to the immediate dismissal of individuals, including the wing commander.

In 1967, McNamara was intent upon reducing the SAC bomber force considerably by 1971. Some B-52E/Fs approached the end of their fatigue lives, accelerated by airborne alert marathons and low-altitude missions in many cases. They were retired and three B-52D squadrons were inactivated. Most of their aircraft were sent to reinforce the units involved in Vietnam *Arc Light* missions, where many crews would complete up to seven TDY combat tours. A new replacement training unit had to be set up within Castle AFB's 4017th CCTS to train crews from other B-52 variants for B-52D flying in South East Asia, as that model was less vital for the deterrent role. It also differed significantly in its electronic and other equipment from the later models. The B-52Ds would be joined by some B-52G units for Operation *Linebacker II*. However, 40 percent of SAC's B-52s were still made available to provide airborne alert and several flew daily airborne alert indoctrination missions.

In 1969, there were still 505 B-52s and 647 KC-135s on strength. Although *Chrome Dome* had recently ended, long range was still a basic requirement and the B-52's much longer legs and greater payload (particularly of stand-off cruise missiles) still counted.

Concerns about their fatigue life were ameliorated by the end of *Chrome Dome* demands and the large numbers of B-52s that were still available.

Decorated with red test aircraft markings and a Snoopy cartoon, B-52G-075-57-6472 releases a Hound Dog during its detachment to Air Materiel Command in 1959. The missile's celestial navigation system locked on to a single star and one missile could cross-feed the star data to the second Hound Dog if necessary. (USAF)

CAMPAIGN OBJECTIVES

Planning Armageddon

B-52B-030-BO 53-0387 (foreground) shares a maintenance area with RB-52B-015-BO 52-8712 and RB-52B-015-BO 52-8714, partially hidden by docks that provided some protection for maintenance work. All three belonged to the 93rd BW at Castle AFB, California in the mid-1950s. (USAF)

Although SAC's motto was "Peace is our Profession," Curtis LeMay never doubted that preserving that peace could require the application of his force's full potential. During the 1962 Cuban Missile Crisis he felt that negotiating with Soviet premier Khrushchev was an inadequate response, commenting that "We are swatting flies when we should be going after the manure pile." Later, as the Vietnam War developed, his biographer claimed that LeMay recommended "bombing North Vietnam back into the Stone Age," a comment that he denied making, although it often defined his reputation. However, he did advocate SAC attacks on Haiphong harbor, crippling the North's wartime re-supply effort. Despite his apparent espousal of the inevitability of nuclear retaliation, with its implicit terminal damage to the entire human race, LeMay's supporters are convinced that he knew that such a catastrophic outcome could never happen, as long as SAC presented a strong deterrent. His successor, Gen Power, expressed the basic tenet of SAC's philosophy, "all the top men of the communist hierarchy, from Lenin to Stalin to Khrushchev, have made it clear that the ultimate goal of communism is the liquidation of capitalist countries and, primarily, of the United States."

In the immediate years following World War II, the USA lacked detailed knowledge of the USSR's industrial and infrastructure sites, so its nuclear planning policy therefore focussed on cities with known industrial resources. It was acknowledged that the Soviet Union's conventional forces substantially outnumbered the West's and that an invasion of Europe could quickly overwhelm the nascent NATO organization, leaving the UK as the only likely base for an Allied response. Early use of SAC's nuclear capability was therefore seen as inevitable to compensate for smaller NATO land forces. Joint Coordination Centers (JCCs) were established in the UK and Tokyo to coordinate atomic combat operations globally.

Direct Soviet air attack on US territory was thought unlikely, until the Soviet Union acquired nuclear weapons. However, conscious of the threat of a Soviet invasion of Europe, the Allies devised a series of war plans in 1948 beginning with Plan *Broiler*, an emergency plan that included nuclear bombing. By May 1948 the JCS had evolved Plan *Halfmoon*,

Battle staff in position aboard a *Looking Glass* EC-135. Early *Looking Glass* versions had only four officers around a small table on the upper deck operating radios and coding devices to communicate with airborne bombers. Later variants carried up to 12 electronics operators, including a SAC missile combat crew (after May 1967, in EC-135Cs) to manage the airborne launch control system for ICBMs. (USAF)

which called for the evacuation of heavily populated areas in Europe and an air campaign that was designed to "exploit the destructive and psychological power of atomic weapons against vital elements of the Soviet war making capacity."

In December 1948, Maj Gen Charles Cabell, Air Staff Director of Intelligence, spoke at the USAF's Exercise *Dualism* conference of the deterrent effect of the atomic bomb. "If a shooting war should come," he warned, "we know that atomic destruction must be delivered to the heartland of the Soviet Union. Only there can Russia be stopped." In Gen LeMay's opinion, this massive destruction should be delivered in a single, coordinated first strike.

Twenty Soviet cities were selected as potential targets, and in June 1948 SAC urgently prepared detailed target folders for them. Further developments in Plan *Darkhorse* required

Vietnam War commitments imposed considerable pressures on SAC resources. B-52s in action amassed impressive mission scores in their long flights from Guam to Vietnamese targets, as seen on the nose of B-52F-070-BW 57-0163. Detached from SIOP duties at the 7th BW at Carswell AFB, Texas to the 320th BW at Andersen AFB, Guam in December 1965, it completed five months of combat operations. (USAF)

A 7th BW alert crew arrives at Hound Dog-carrying B-52F-070-BW 57-0176 on Carswell AFB's hardstanding in 1967. Alert crews ran from the "molehole" to their crew vehicles and the first to arrive usually became the driver, although gunners often performed this and other support duties. (Terry Panopalis collection)

most of the missions to be flown from continental American (CONUS) bases and those in mainland Europe to pre-empt the time delays associated with operating from forward bases and transporting nuclear weapons and other supplies to them ahead of an attack.

For closer access to likely targets, SAC's August 1948 Plan *Fleetwood* (updating *Halfmoon*) envisaged its bombers using British-operated bases in Egypt. Quickly seen as impractical, it was replaced by Plan *Trojan* for which B-29s would fly from the UK and Okinawa, supported by B-36s from American locations. When the UK's considerable V-bomber force became operational from 1954, a joint plan with SAC envisaged the RAF V-bombers launching first and reaching Soviet targets before SAC aircraft could arrive on target.

The discovery on September 3, 1949 that the Soviet Union was conducting atomic weapon tests lent urgency to the task. The US government's Joint Strategic Planning Committee then turned to North Africa as an additional basing area in Plan *Offtackle*. Ben Guerir and Sidi Slimane in French Morocco were suitable for bombers, providing the shortest distances for them to attack Soviet targets and return to base. Over 300 bombers and support aircraft would also deploy to British forward bases. *Offtackle*'s aim was to ensure the "destruction of vital elements in the enemy war-making capacity and the retardation of enemy advances in western Eurasia." Transportation nets, armament factories, and oil processing facilities would be hit by 292 atomic bombs, assuming that the 1948 total of around 50 in the armory had been significantly increased within a year. These attacks would constitute the USA's only offensive operations at the start of a war initiated by the USSR. The Plan also estimated SAC attrition in those attacks, calculating that up to a third of the bombers would not reach their targets and, of those that did, over a half would be seriously damaged or lost.

Forward deployments of B-47Bs and nuclear bombs to UK bases began in the early 1950s with Operation *Sky Try*, a US-based full-scale simulated combat test. Fifteen 306th BW B-47Bs and their KC-97E tankers then flew to RAF Fairford, England in June 1953 for 90 days, starting a pattern of SAC deployments to Mildenhall, Upper Heyford and Brize-Norton in the UK. Entire wings took part until 1958. The 321st BW was typical in making five B-47 deployments to Morocco between 1954 and 1961. However, the idea of prolonged overseas basing was undermined in 1953 by a RAND analysis that bombers in Europe and North Africa would be unacceptably vulnerable to a Soviet first strike. LeMay then conceded that the bases would be better used to recover aircraft post-strike and refuel them for further action. This idea was tested in the 1954 Operation *Quick Strike*.

SAC then reduced the logistical burden by sending a few aircraft from each wing on shorter *Reflex* visits from 1958. From June 1954, bombers on alert duty and exercises were usually armed with nuclear weapons. Other bombers would fly as decoys or jammers in the assault waves. B-47Bs with 1,700-gallon external tanks could fly missions within a 1,704-mile radius, extended by in-flight refueling if tankers were available. Tests with B-47s armed with Mk 21 bombs involved eight-hour missions with an initial 300-mile run at 500ft altitude and a "pop-up" to 20,000ft for release. While the low-altitude penetration run provided some protection from enemy defenses, the pop-up exposed the bomber closer to the target where missiles and guns would be most numerous. Lower-altitude lay-down techniques were also devised for B-52s.

SAC expansion

LeMay, who wanted instant control over his organization in an international emergency, ensured that SAC was a completely self-sufficient command with its own tankers, escort fighters, reconnaissance, and transport squadrons. He received the new C-97 and C-124 transport aircraft before the USAF's dedicated Military Air Transport Service (MATS) and regularly deployed SAC F-84G Thunderjet fighter units to North Africa and the UK to protect his bombers. SAC strategic reconnaissance with RB-17s, RB-29s, and RB-50Es began in 1948, and by 1952 overflights of Soviet territory were being made by RB-45Cs, some flown by RAF crews. Expansion continued throughout the 1950s with six new bombardment wings, four strategic reconnaissance wings, and two tanker wings, in addition to extra fighter and transport units, between 1953 and 1955 alone. In 1958, B-47 wings each added a fourth squadron to cope with alert and *Reflex Action* requirements.

SAC, which had 683 tankers by late 1954, also asserted that in-flight refueling had become "as important to SAC global operations as are take-offs and landings." This was demonstrated further in two December 1956 two-week exercises, *Power House* and *Road Block*, in which 1,000 bombers and forward-deployed tankers flew simulated combat strikes over North America and the Arctic.

By 1955, SAC's options had become more complex. LeMay believed that the opportunity to potentially beat the Soviets with minimal SAC attrition, when "their defenses were pretty weak," had passed. The Weapons Systems Evaluation Group (WSEG) calculated that it would now require a force twice as large as SAC's to destroy all known Soviet bases. The Killian Committee warned that "We have an offensive advantage but are vulnerable to surprise attack." Three years later, a pre-emptive strike, after warning, was seen as the only

93rd BW RB-52B-015-BO 52-8715 displays an early placement of the SAC sash in February 1956. "Peace is Our Profession" became SAC's motto, but it originally read "Maintaining Peace is Our Profession." When a painter was asked to display the words on a board to advertise a 1957 USAF re-enlistment drive, there was insufficient space to fit in the whole sentence. Col Charles Van Vliet, the 8th AF Director of Information, liked the shorter slogan and it became standard. Humorists often added "war is just our hobby." (Terry Panopalis collection)

way to prevent a devastating Soviet nuclear assault, although Eisenhower ruled out that possibility. The threat of massive retaliation continued as the basis of US strategy. LeMay believed that refusing to make the first strike would put SAC at a severe disadvantage in trying to launch a counterattack after losing a considerable proportion of its assets. "Our only other defense," he said, "is to know when the attack is coming so, at best, you won't be there when it hits you."

The Killian Report ("Meeting the Threat of Surprise Attack"), published in February 1955 by the USAF's Science Advisory Panel, exacerbated US alarm at the bomber gap, the supposed numerical superiority of Soviet bomber forces to those of the USA. It suggested that the Soviet threat was far greater than planners had envisaged and that there would be over 1,000 nuclear-capable bombers in Soviet service by 1959. The eventual revelation via U-2 surveillance from 1956 that this was a fallacy generated understandable opposition to the rapid expansion of US offensive capability. However, forceful proponents of airpower such as LeMay were still able to preserve contracts for the big bomber programs in place and introduce improved B-52 versions.

Finding targets

In 1959 it was decided that a national strategic targeting list (NSTL) should be developed, complete with desired ground zeros (DGZs), or target coordinates for each objective. A year later the plan included the matching of targets with individual aircraft, allowing for air defenses, weapons effects, and likely risks associated with penetration routes. Alert aircraft took priority as the first on target. During mission briefing, SAC navigators studied defense intelligence target reconnaissance (DTIR) photos of targets, many taken by U-2s before their flights were ended following the shooting down of Gary Powers in May 1960. Target lists determined the number of weapons ordered by SAC, which in turn influenced procurement of appropriate numbers of bombers.

During the 1950s, aerial reconnaissance became the principal method of trying to define the true strength of Soviet forces in an increasingly tense climate of threats from Moscow. Although SAC's most significant additions were the B-52 from June 1955 and the KC-135 aerial refueler in 1957, the RB-52B, developed alongside the B-52A bomber, greatly increased SAC's long-range reconnaissance capability on trans-Arctic missions. However, only 27 were built and bombs often replaced the two-man pressurized capsule installed in the bomb-bay for photographic or ECM missions. From 1956, the RB-52B was supplemented by Martin RB-57Ds. Reconnaissance B-47 versions were far more numerous with 290 built in several versions. Project *Homerun* from March 21 to May 10, 1956 saw 26th SRW and 55th SRW RB-47E/Hs forward based at Thule AB, Greenland flying regular 3,400-mile electronic and photographic missions over the northern interior of the Soviet Union.

RB-57s were replaced by SAC's most innovative and long-serving reconnaissance aircraft, the Lockheed U-2. It enabled direct overflights of the Soviet bloc, rather than relying on reconnaissance flights that flew close to the border and acquired their intelligence by peering over it with 100in. focal length cameras. The U-2 entered CIA service covertly early in 1956, managed by SAC. SAC's own 4080th SRW received U-2As the following year in June 1957.

A 1958 report by political scientist Albert Wohlstetter at the influential RAND institute entitled "The Delicate Balance of Terror" emphasized the vulnerability of SAC's bases and ICBM silos to Soviet missiles. It led to a 1959 report estimating that most of the tankers and bombers would be eliminated in the first strike waves. The obvious, though hugely expensive, solution was to keep a proportion of the bomber force in the air at all times, with others on ground alert so that they could be quickly sent into action.

By 1960, SAC had 12 heavy bombardment wings controlling over 580 B-52s and 25 medium bomber wings with 1,178 B-47s. Some were available for *Reflex Action* operations which deployed aircraft to forward bases, or on earlier 90-day rotations involving 45 aircraft. Gen Power told his SAC personnel in November 1967 that their demanding commitment to an effective alert posture was vital because "we can expect the Soviets to use the oldest and most successful military stratagem – surprise, because they would surely want to exploit our weaknesses, not our strengths. The only way of ensuring the survival of some of SAC's combat capability, even in the case of the most unexpected and massive attack, is our Alert Force."

SIOP

Soon after taking office in 1960, President John F. Kennedy ordered SAC's 15-minute ground alert to extend to half its force to provide a stronger deterrent posture. In July 1961, this goal was attained. The superior ability of SAC bombers, ICBMs and submarine-launched ballistic missiles (SLBM) led to the development, in 1960, of the Single Integrated Operational Plan (SIOP) which set out a massive, complex US plan (it required nine tons of paperwork) for conducting nuclear warfare. Initially requested by Eisenhower and executed by Gen Power, it was introduced in July 1961 for the fiscal year 1962 (SIOP-62), at a time when the USA had over 3,200 nuclear warheads, and it continued in various forms until 2003. It included a National Target Base (NTB), which, at the height of the Cold War, detailed up to 16,000 targets in the Russian Federation, North Korea, Iraq, and other potentially hostile states. Of these, 2,220 were priority targets and 835 were air defense sites that would be attacked by Hound Dogs.

SIOP also specified how many nuclear weapons were allocated to each target and it envisaged delivering them all in one massive wave of bombers and missiles to neutralize all enemy nuclear forces. Coordination of times over targets (TOT) for all the potential delivery, including ICBMs and the RAF V-Force, was a particularly complex, ongoing problem. The commander in chief of SAC was responsible for Strategic Target Planning.

Targets in the Sino-Soviet bloc were allocated 7,847 megatons of destruction. A defense executive who questioned the apportionment of 40 megatons to Moscow alone

A rare moment of amity between Cold War crises. Nikita Khrushchev (left) meets President Eisenhower (second right) during an 11-day goodwill visit to the USA in September 1959. Within a year, the goodwill had evaporated after the shoot-down of Francis Gary Powers' U-2 spyplane. (Public Domain)

B-52 production was accelerated in the late 1950s in response to the supposed bomber gap in numbers compared with the USSR's bomber fleet. The forward fuselage of B-52C-045-BO 54-2668 is about to be joined to Section 43, the center fuselage, at Boeing's Seattle factory. It was completed by August 31, 1956 and delivered to the 42nd BW at Loring AFB, Maine on 9 September. (USAF).

was reassured that it was quite enough. Gen Power argued against accusations of overkill, pointing out that attrition would neutralize more enemy weapons. Others stated that an onslaught on communist China, integral to SIOP-62, did not allow for the possibility that it was "not their war." Power replied that removing China from targeting "would really screw up the plan."

SAC policy, in the era of Mutually Assured Destruction (MAD) was always to threaten a massive first strike as the true deterrent to any level of nuclear assault. SIOP-63 modified the number of warheads or bombs that would be delivered on a single target (some were allocated up to five) so that nuclear fallout on friendly nations could be reduced if a target appeared to be sufficiently degraded by a first strike. A list of around 40 prime city targets had, in fact, existed since 1945. As the Cold War deepened and SIOP went through many changes, that list expanded to 840 targets requiring over 3,000 nuclear weapons. Any remaining enemy capability after such a hellish barrage could be tackled via flexible response options.

The policy also gave Washington a greater role in controlling military actions, including nuclear retaliation. During the Bay of Pigs misadventure and the subsequent Cuban Missile Crisis, Kennedy had to battle with the more forceful members of the JCS in order to avoid outright nuclear conflict with the Soviet Union. His flexible response doctrine, relevant primarily to the European context, gave him more authority to restrain those belligerent attitudes. It provided for more limited attacks on selected bomber and missile bases, leaving the threat of an all-out nuclear "massive retaliation" as a deterrent. Flexible response, described in SIOP-63 in 1961, evolved into a policy to deter Soviet inroads into Europe for which Kennedy's advisors wanted greatly increased conventional forces. He requested an extra $3.25 billion for them and for putting more bombers on ground alert as a second strike force to follow up missile attacks. Airborne alert was not included in these early SIOP plans.

McNamara budgeted for nuclear forces, as a SIOP triad would destroy the enemy's military forces, but also a quarter of the civilian population as "collateral damage" in a deterrent policy of "assured destruction." Its final stage on both sides would be an automatic, timed launch of a final strike that would be programmed to happen even after the deaths of all the missile operators.

Early B-52s such as this RB-52B-010-BO (52-0012), the 14th production aircraft, were used for training at Castle AFB, California in this case until November 1965. Open bomb-bay doors reveal elements of the complex reconnaissance equipment. The first production B-52s were costed at $25m each, but this fell to $7.5m when mass production was under way. (USAF).

B-52H 60-0022 at Boeing, Wichita awaits delivery to the 4136th BW at the start of a career that would take it well into the 21st century. (Terry Panopalis collection)

In 1962 the USA had around 3,500 available nuclear weapons compared with the USSR's 300–500 (158 of them in Cuba), but the use of even a few would have been devastating to both sides. Fortunately, neither leader had any real intention of starting a nuclear war, although the possibility of escalation started by accidents or mistakes by individuals remained, as seen in the shooting down of a U-2 over Cuba by an impulsive and misinformed Soviet general. *Chrome Dome* airborne alert B-52 crews were told on October 24 to look out for any nuclear detonations. Since none of them had ever seen one, it was hoped that a misinterpreted lightning flash would not trigger a nuclear holocaust.

Flexible response implied the use of bombers. Unlike missiles they could be adapted to carry conventional weapons for a limited conflict. In the nuclear scenario, they could be recalled minutes before being committed to attack a target. A nuclear-tipped ICBM could not be disarmed or self-destruct after launch. By the mid-1970s, defenders of the bomber concept argued that B-52s armed with cruise missiles (which the United States hoped to exempt from the ongoing SALT talks) would be able to avoid the worst of Soviet defenses. If the then-canceled Rockwell B-1A was reinstated it could make low altitude, supersonic first strikes on strategic targets followed up by cruise missiles such as the Tomahawk (or, later, the AGM-86) launched at a relatively safe distance by B-52s.

President Carter accepted that cruise missiles on B-52s would be a reasonable trade-off with SAC for canceling the B-1A. The addition of terrain contour matching (TERCOM) guidance would make the missiles far more accurate than their predecessors, some of which, such as the SM-62 ground-launched Snark, were notoriously inaccurate. Lacking a new bomber, the USAF turned to the proposed MX missile, a much more powerful "silo-busting" successor to Minuteman as a response to the improved, more accurate Soviet SS-18 and mobile SS-20, each of which contained up to 14 warheads. The enormous cost of MX and the impossibility of establishing mobile launch points to avoid a Soviet first strike made it wholly impractical. For SAC bombers the B53 nine-megaton "bunker buster" weapon was an effective destroyer of silos or underground command centers. Developed in 1962, it could be dropped with accuracy at altitudes below 200ft in laydown mode with a three-minute delayed action and several retarding parachutes, using a "pitch up and pull over" maneuver.

THE CAMPAIGN

The long patrol

Buff riders

Increased airborne alert missions began immediately after President Kennedy's October 22, 1962 speech revealing the presence of Soviet missiles on Cuba. The 4228th SW at Columbus AFB, Michigan was among the first to get a pair of B-52Fs airborne with four B28F-1 bombs aboard. The unit was operating an alert pattern of three days' ground alert followed by a *Chrome Dome* mission. (USAF)

A basic B-52 crew had six members: two pilots (aircraft commander and co-pilot), a radar navigator and radar navigator, an electronic warfare officer (EW or "E-Dub"), and an enlisted man as tail gunner. In flight, crew members referred to each other over the intercom by their crew position; "pilot," "nav," "radar," etc. Up to three additional instructor crew members could be carried in the cramped space. They were provided with jump seats, one of which was also the lower deck "honey bucket," rather than the vital but famously uncomfortable ejection seats. The instructor/navigator's seat was the worst: a fold-down "shelf" at the rear of the "black hole." A tail gunner had to jettison his entire gun assembly in an emergency and then jump out. When the B-52G/H gunner made a welcome move to a forward cabin position with an ejection seat he operated his four .50 Browning machine guns (or 20mm M61 cannon in the B-52H) remotely with a radar-directed MD-9 fire control system.

The EW role became more important as enemy electronic defenses became more sophisticated. In addition, on *Chrome Domes*, EWs had to monitor, decode, authenticate, and respond to frequent, detailed HF radio messages from *Sky King*, *Democrat* or other SAC *Giant Talk* system communications. ECM training, however, was slower to evolve, as EW technician Pete S. Kuehl observed. "On training missions, we always had runs against ECM sites scattered all over the USA. With the primitive receivers they had at the time [1940s-era AN/APR9 and APR-14 sets] I don't know how they handled those runs without prior knowledge of the frequencies to expect."

The crew boarded through the lower crew door, ascending a three-rung ladder adjacent to the lower crew compartment to reach the flight deck. The navigator and radar navigator remained below in a small, dark lower compartment (the black hole), sitting in downward-firing Weber ejection seats surrounded by a mass of electronic equipment. They were the first to bail out and any extra crew bailed out through the open spaces left by their ejection seats.

American forces were put on high stages of alert status on three occasions during the Cold War. One of the earliest occasions for B-52 units occurred in November 1956 during

The dual punch of a nuclear payload and AGM-28 Hound Dogs was a credible deterrent throughout the *Chrome Dome* era. The AGM-28A inventory totaled 593 units by 1963, most of them modified to AGM-28Bs with a reduced radar signature. (USAF)

the Suez Crisis. B-52Bs had entered service with the 93rd BW in June 1955 and two more bombardment wings, the 42nd BW and 99th BW were converting from the B-36 and B-47 respectively. The USA did not become involved directly, but as a demonstration of SAC's ability to respond to any emergency worldwide a KC-97 tanker force was sent north to bases in Greenland, Labrador, and Newfoundland. A B-47 wing in the UK and a B-36 unit on Guam were put on alert.

At that time the newly introduced B-52B force organized a series of long-distance flights in Operation *Quick Kick*. One 93rd BW B-52B (53-388) commanded by Col Marcus Hill stayed aloft for 31.5 hours, covering 13,500nm and needing four KC-97 tanker join-ups. Operation *Power Flite* in mid-January 1957 was another carefully planned demonstration of what would later be known as SAC's "global reach." In LeMay's words, it showed "SAC's capabilities to strike any target on the face of the earth." Three 93rd BW B-52Bs, with pre-positioned KC-97s in North Africa and the Philippines, completed a 24,325-mile flight around the world in 45 hours 19 minutes. KC-135s would have reduced the time by six hours. The wing won the Mackay Trophy for this endurance test and one tail gunner, Airman Preiss (with a pile of books for entertainment), broke an unofficial record by becoming the first person to fly around the world backwards. Other record flights left the Soviet Union in no doubt about its vulnerability to B-52 incursions from anywhere along its borders.

Chrome Dome begins

During the 1950s, Americans increasingly believed that the Soviet Union was the main threat to their otherwise prosperous postwar lives. A 1957 report entitled "Deterrence and Survival in the Nuclear Age" recommended that SAC should be put on constant alert. The *Chrome Dome* policy, or Airborne Alert Indoctrination program, was a logical continuation of the ground alert policy begun in 1955 and it was triggered in 1958 by anxiety about the apparent expansion of Soviet ICBM assets. Gen Power, architect of the airborne alert

Immaculate in its radiation-resistant finish, with further white areas to cool the cabin and electronic bays, B-52H-155-BW 60-0049 displays its 449th Bomb Wing patch on its nose at Kincheloe AFB, Michigan. Its original "owners," the 4042nd SW, were renumbered as the 449th BW in February 1963 and the 93rd Bomb Squadron became the 716th BS to honor a famous World War II B-24 Liberator unit. (USAF)

strategy, had revealed in November 1957 that, in addition to ground alert, he had "a certain percentage of my command in the air. These planes are bombed up and they don't carry bows and arrows." Journalists deduced that he implied that nuclear weapons were aboard those sentinels which had been on airborne alert since September 15 carrying safer "sealed pit" weapons, sanctioned by the president, where the nuclear core was already in place rather than having to be inserted in flight.

A *Chrome Dome* mission began with take-off at around 450,000lb (for a B-52F), flying a predetermined route to an orbit point in international airspace near the Soviet border where the pilot flew racetrack patterns in full view of Soviet radars. They remained on station until relieved by another B-52, or they could deliver a retaliatory nuclear second strike if necessary.

Crews usually flew four 24-hour missions, midday to midday, with one week's break after the fourth flight. However, as Col Phil Rowe recalled, "The Lebanon Crisis and the Cuban missile fiasco were two of the toughest periods for SAC crews. Some pulled 45 days of continuous alert for the former, but most believed that chances of an actual war mission scramble were greater during the latter period of tension." His crew flew 28 *Chrome Dome* missions over a seven-month period. B-52H crews from the 319th BW(H) at Grand Forks, North Dakota sometimes flew 36-hour *Chrome Domes.*

On a *Chrome Dome* two crew members including a pilot had to be awake at any given time, but careful scheduling of crew rest times aboard usually allowed all personnel the chance of eight hours' sleep during the mission. "The plan, intended for when one pilot was asleep, was that one non-pilot could sit up front to keep the other pilot awake and help monitor things." As an EWO, Phil Rowe was given some flight simulator training so that he could be that pilot watcher.

Airborne alert had its origins in the *Head Start I* tests run by the 42nd BW at Loring AFB, Maine from September 15 to December 15, 1958. Sealed-pit Mk 15 Mod 2 or Mk 39 Mod 1 weapons were loaded for March 1959 *Head Start* tests on 24-hour airborne alert flights over the Arctic region. In July 1959 when Gen Power told Congress that, to deny the Soviet Union the element of surprise, "I feel strongly that we must get on with airborne alert. We must impress Mr Khrushchev that we have it and that he cannot strike this country with impunity." His request for a regular airborne alert commitment was turned down, but a full-time training program called Airborne Alert Indoctrination was allowed to proceed.

As the policy spread through 11 SAC wings it assumed various titles including *Wirebrush* and Operation *Coverall*, which required airborne alert sorties to fly over designated areas

A B28F1 nuclear bomb is unloaded from a B-52H. As a primary weapon for *Chrome Dome* and NATO use from 1962 to 1972, its design prioritized reduced size compared with early weapons. With an external diameter of only 20in., the 170in.-long B28 weighed 2,040lb. The B28F1 was a lay-down version for B-52s attacking at 500ft altitude with a retarding parachute. (USAF)

of the Atlantic and Pacific Oceans towards the Canadian Arctic (with permission from Canada), but they were limited to a few bombers at a time in a reduced "1/39th Alert" pattern. Gen Power announced on January 18, 1961 that airborne alert training, involving combat ready aircrews, was happening at 24 SAC bases. In fact, almost 6,000 missions had already been flown. Initially, a single, armed B-52 was launched for airborne alert on four separate occasions within 24 hours, but when all 11 wings were involved by November 1961 12 *Chrome Dome* sorties were launched daily. In some wings the commitment was lower. The 320th BW had to launch one nuclear-armed B-52 per day for a month during its turn on the airborne alert rota in 1962, while keeping eight more on ground alert. At its peak, a quarter of each unit flew airborne alerts, but operational considerations and cost reduced this by half.

A battery of 0.50 M-3 guns receives attention. Its complex ammunition feed and spent case ejection systems often caused jams, but it could be effective against intercepting fighters at up to 3,500ft range with a combined rate of fire of 3,000 rounds. (USAF)

The number could be increased considerably, given three days' warning to prepare extra bombers and crews. Early in the program, airborne alert duties were rotated between units, giving each one three weeks on duty, about twice annually. During its duty period each crew usually flew about four *Chrome Domes*. However, there would be several crises that would greatly increase that commitment. By 1967, four groups of four bomb wings were on the *Chrome Dome* schedule with each group providing four missions daily for a six-week period.

By January 18, 1961 when the program was publicly announced, 6,000 airborne alert "training sorties" had already been flown. They evolved into longer flightpaths over the northern polar region and into the Mediterranean (the southern or Spanish *Chrome Dome*), which allowed far more bombers to be managed and air-refueled at various stages along them. The *Chrome Dome* title allegedly referred to the baldness generated by wearing a ten-pound flying helmet for over 24 hours, or more idealistically to the idea of a protective dome of many silver-painted airborne B-52s.

Additional in-flight refueling could have extended the 24-hour missions, but the B-52's oil reserves could not keep the engines lubricated for much longer than that. The endurance of a crew in such confined conditions was also a major factor. While much of a *Chrome Dome* flight was managed by the autopilot, allowing several members to nap, a low-altitude leg required constant, intense concentration and effective teamwork by the whole crew for prolonged periods. During the tedious on-station orbits one pilot could try to sleep for a while, despite the noise and constant movement, in the narrow bunk. His seat would be temporarily occupied by another crew member. Dehydration was a hazard of prolonged high-altitude flight and airsickness was common. Air conditioning was unreliable, particularly in the B-52D. Heavy insulated flight gear was worn for northern route *Chrome Domes* in case of bail-out over Arctic terrain, so cabin temperatures had to be reduced accordingly.

A six-man crew from the 525th BS heads for B-52H-145-BW 60-0032 in 1962. A 24-hour *Chrome Dome* mission was preceded by up to six hours of preparation and two hours of debriefing, taking crews to their limits of endurance. This was a factor in ending the missions in 1968, as was the increasing movement of B-52 crews into Vietnam war units. Crews in units such as the 68th BW flew a *Chrome Dome* roughly every ten days. (USAF)

Initially, President Kennedy asked for 12 B-52s to be present on *Chrome Dome* routes, far fewer than the 70 that SAC desired. Each unit allocated one or two B-52s daily and those aircraft received maximum care and attention from their maintainers to minimize "aborts." On a northerly *Chrome Dome* route at over 40,000ft the bombers passed through air temperatures of around -60°F and over similar ground temperatures. Crews knew that a high-altitude ejection would give them virtually no chance of survival. Neither the sun nor the moon was visible at those northerly positions, as the navigator worked from Grid Navigation maps in an area where magnetic compasses told you that north was south due to polar magnetic interference. They relied on the aircraft's gyroscopes to maintain the correct heading and on old-fashioned dead-reckoning and celestial navigation. For the latter, the navigator asked the ECM officer to "shoot" star positions with a periscope sextant extending from an access port above his crew position.

Staying on course in these conditions required constant attention from both navigators, leaving them little rest time. Fortunately, inertial navigation systems in later B-52s alleviated these problems. Unexpected high-altitude jet winds, violent turbulence, and the general lack of recognizable ground features added to the difficulties. Navigators spent two hours preparing for each hour of flight, although basic timing and flight plan information was usually "canned" for *Chrome Dome* routes.

Clearly, the success of *Chrome Dome* relied on the availability of tankers. The first major demonstration of the bomber–tanker team was organized in mid-October 1958 for the three days of Operation *Fast Move*. Seventy KC-135As joined 86 KC-97s at Canadian and northeastern American locations to provided fuel for 29 B-52s and 164 B-47s, dispersed at their alert bases. Northern route *Chrome Dome* tankers usually operated from Goose Bay, Labrador. The long-distance flights soon added to crews' total flight hours. One 95th BW B-52B crew member from Biggs AFB, Texas accumulated 2,800 hours in six years from 1960, many of them on *Chrome Dome* flights. Three-week TDY *Reflex* trips to Guam were also required regularly for Biggs crews.

In one mission profile, pairs of bombers on the northern *Chrome Dome* route at a cruise altitude of around 32,000ft made their first tanker rendezvous on the *Black Goat* refueling track off Newfoundland. This first encounter signalled the warming of the day's first frozen ready meal in the small B-52 galley. The route then continued north across the Arctic Circle over Baffin Bay, Thule AB in Greenland (the most northerly US base), and a series of racetrack patterns over the inhospitable Arctic ice mass. Each orbit lasted around 30 minutes covering 250 miles in each direction, totaling eight or nine tedious hours "on station."

Then to Point Barrow in Alaska, for a second refueling session by a tanker from Eielson AFB, Alaska on the *Cold Coffee* refueling track after almost 18 hours of monotonous flying on autopilot with only the aurora borealis for entertainment for those crew members with external vision. This took them closer to the 192 islands of the Franz Josef Land peninsula, housing the Soviet Union's most northerly military base. At that point, EWs could tune in to listen to Soviet radar operators conversing. Later, *Chrome Dome* routes tended to fly their patrols slightly further south to avoid the possibility of navigation problems that might take them into Soviet airspace. A variation, the western route, took B-52s from the US west coast on a return flight north of Alaska twice daily.

Most of the flight was on autopilot and there was a separate, smaller set of extra throttles for autopilot flight with two knobs controlling engines four and five. Slight adjustments were sufficient to set the speed to the exact figure required. The pilots then spent most of their time checking the 40 engine instruments, fuel gauges, and other important dials to check for any anomalies, adjusting the center of gravity with the smaller throttles as fuel burned off. The co-pilot also had to check on the distant tail gunner in B-52B/F versions.

When the bombers reached their orbit stations, they were at the shortest possible distance from their targets, which became the quickest way, apart from ICBMs, to deliver a retaliatory strike. Their sorties followed two basic routes. The southern route (so called because it began over the southern USA) crossed the Atlantic and Spain, picking up the TACAN beacon at Santiago, and then traversed the Mediterranean, from which point targets in the south of the Soviet Union could be approached if necessary. Radio check-ins had to be made near Italy (Roma Control), Malta, and other points en route, and there was also the occasional risk of interception by Libyan fighters. Some crews were aware that radar surveillance aircraft were following their progress across the Mediterranean and they were frequently subjected to electronic interference from Soviet spy trawlers and false messages from hostile ground stations.

Two refueling sessions were provided over Spain by tankers from Moron or Torrejon, Spain. The first came seven hours into the mission over the Pyrenees, when each B-52 received around 110,000lb of fuel, and the second on the return trip after 14 hours.

2

3

SOUTH CAROLINA

Columbia

EVENTS

1 23 January 1961: 1056hrs: *Keep 19* takes off from Seymour-Johnson AFB on a 24-hour *Chrome Dome* qualifying flight. Two MK-39 sealed pit nuclear bombs are aboard. Flight refueling occurs at 1600hrs in good weather although the aircraft is exhibiting electrical and internal fuel transfer problems.

2 2100hrs: *Keep 19* meets KC-135A *Addle 57* for a second refueling session at 29,000ft near Columbia, NC. After a few seconds, the refueling boom is disconnected due to exceeding movement limits between the aircraft. Three more disconnects occur at 260kts as 93,000lb of fuel are transferred. The boom operator reports fuel leaks from the B-52's right wing.

3 24 January 1961: 0930hrs: No.4 fuel gauge shows heavy fuel loss of 36 gallons per sec due to a rupture in the right wing integral fuel tank. *Addle 57* crew move in behind the bomber to see where the leak is from. Major Tulloch heads for Seymour-Johnson with *Addle 57* a mile ahead. The crews leave the refueling track and divert to sea, crossing the coast at Wilmington, NC. Pump failure prevents No.3 fuel tank from emptying fuel.

4 *Keep 19* and *Addle 57* orbit ten miles offshore at 30,000ft and the B-52's No.5 and 6 engines (right, inboard pair) are shut down. Sgt. Barnish enters the bomb bay and finds fuel cascading into the bay, electronics, and landing gear. The B-52's ARAC 58 HF radio is failing.

5 2330hrs: Tulloch attempts to return to base. The aircraft appears to be under control, but metal fatigue is rapidly widening a crack in a panel of wing section 556. Fuel line connectors are also weakening.

6 Descending to 10,000ft, an emergency lowering of the landing gear is performed 40 miles south of Seymour-Johnson AFB. At 9,000ft, Tulloch lowers the flaps. He turns the bomber onto a 260-degree heading to line up with Runway 26 for an instrument landing (ILS) approach at 180kts.

7 The right wing begins to fracture, causing an uncontrollable turn to the right. Engines on the left wing are cut and the two engines on the right are accelerated but the turn continues. Loud noises are heard and the right wing fails, folding up and over the aircraft as it rolls inverted and begins to break up.

8 Tulloch ejects and lands in Nahunta Swamp. Rardin lands near Bull Head Bridge. Shelton's body is found in a tree near Rardin's landing, fatally injured in a collision with the ejection seat. Wilson lands near Fort Run Road and breaks his ankle. Brown, first to eject, lands near Wilson. Mattocks escapes through the cockpit and deploys his parachute seconds before the aircraft explodes. Barnish and Richards' bodies are found in the wreckage on Big Daddy's Road.

9 Bomb No. 1 (6,750lbs, 3.8 megaton yield) is suspended in a tree with six of the seven stages of nuclear detonation completed. The ARM/SAFE switch has not been activated so it remains at SAFE.

10 Bomb No. 2 hits the ground at 700mph and penetrates 18ft into the Nahunta Swamp. Its potential "kill zone" would have extended for 17 miles.

The Goldsboro *Broken Arrow*

This is the journey of B-52G *Keep 19* and its crash on approach to Seymour-Johnson AFB, North Carolina near Goldsboro, with the loss of two nuclear weapons, one of which came close to exploding and destroying large areas of the USA. The crew comprised: Major Walter S Tulloch (commander), Capt. Richard W Rardin (co-pilot), 1/Lt William R Wilson (EW officer), Capt. Paul E Brown (nav/bombardier), TSgt Francis R Barnish (gunner), Major Eugene H Richards (EW supervisor), Major Gene Shelton (radar navigator), and 1/Lt Adam C Mattocks (3rd pilot).

NORTH CAROLINA
1
Goldsboro
7
6
8
Nahunta Swamp
9
10
Jacksonville
5
California Beach
4

The dubious comfort of the rarely used single bunk was also available in later B-52s for those who could tolerate sleeping in one position, but the floor was the more usual bed. Despite its size, the B-52's crew accommodation was cramped. All, apart from the pilot and co-pilot, worked in "black holes," including the gunner in B-52G/H models. The short ladder from the lower compartment to the flight deck was the only place where one could stand up. (USAF)

The assigned emergency recovery base was in Morocco. *Chrome Dome* assignments were rotated around the B-52 wings and some wings specialized in one of them. For example, the 416th BW at Griffiss AFB, New York flew the southern route, although it was often allocated *Thule Monitors* as well. Its B-52Gs regularly carried four 1.1 megaton bombs, Quails, and two Hound Dogs for these flights. Tanker crews rotated in and out of the Alaska, Spain or northeast USA tanker forces on 45- to 60-day cycles.

The northern route took bombers up the eastern coast of Canada and close to the North Pole before returning along the west coast of the USA. Both routes avoided large population centers en route to a mainly over-water flight. By 1962, eight B-52s were flying the northern route and four took the southern (Mediterranean) route. They usually carried two Hound Dogs and four nuclear weapons. As Gen Power commented, it was a deterrent approach which "never has been attempted in the military history of the world before."

During the Cuban Missile Crisis DEFCON-3 was enforced on October 22,1962 after President Kennedy revealed the presence of Soviet missiles in Cuba. By 2222hrs on October 23, one-eighth of SAC's bombers were in the air carrying nuclear weapons (four Mk 28s or two Mk 15/Mk 39s) with full tanker support, delivering up to 14,000,000lb of fuel for 70 *Chrome Dome* sorties daily. At its peak, when DEFCON-2 was declared and all SAC forces were generated by October 26, 75 sorties were launched daily: 42 on the northern route and 31 on the southern, supported by 38 KC-135As from Spain. KC-135s flew 133 sorties in one day including *Blue Banner* missions to track Soviet ships, with others contributed by the KC-97 fleet. Khrushchev believed that 20 percent of all SAC aircraft was airborne at any time. During one month of the Cuban Crisis, B-52s flew 2,088 *Chrome Dome* sorties totaling 47,168 flying hours. On November 4, 1962, 76 nuclear-armed B-52s and 138 KC-135s were involved in *Chrome Dome* missions. After the crisis passed, SAC still maintained 12 airborne alert B-52s on patrol around Soviet borders. The deterrent effect had worked, as was obvious from Khrushchev's later decisions to back down and withdraw his weapons from Cuba.

In all, 208 aircraft were directly involved and within the requirements of SIOP-63 and SAC's basic Strike Plan 50-63 this meant that a 15-aircraft unit was expected to provide 15 SIOP sorties and two for *Chrome Dome* at any time. There were 1,479 bombers and 2,952 nuclear warheads in the inventory, although the more advanced types with multiple fusing options were not yet available. Their potential target list included 220 Task 1 high-priority military and industrial sites, including the Kremlin. Soviet nuclear missiles placed in Cuba were theoretically capable of hitting 34 of SAC's 76 bomber bases as well as city targets, although only a few of the SS-4 missiles were ready for action when the crisis ended.

B-47 units, many of which were close to retiring their aircraft, were also called in, including the 509th BW from Pease AFB, New Hampshire, which relocated to Logan Airport, Boston and set up operations in the Air National Guard office. Food, accommodation, fuel, and security had to be arranged locally, but the morning after arrival it was found that the B-47Es' landing gear had sunk into the surface of their dispersal area requiring assistance from heavy tow-trucks before operations could begin.

Moles

Aircrew involved in early *Chrome Dome* and other alert missions (including those by B-47s) were often accommodated for around four days in trailers within barbed-wire enclosures near the take-off end of the runway, from which they could easily reach their bombers when the ear-splitting klaxons sounded throughout the base. From 1961, purpose-built, two-storey, ground-alert facilities, with an underground living storey accessed by a sloping tunnel (hence the nickname "moleholes"), were built at SAC bases. They offered good 24-hour catering facilities, two-man bedrooms, a recreation room, dispensary, and a cinema doubling as a briefing space for eight crews.

There were also opportunities, in more relaxed periods, for practical jokes, strong coffee, and high-stakes card games, but no alcohol. Tanker "toads" and bomber crews had separate areas within the facility, but all had to remain in the "alert pad" on instant readiness for the duration of their alert period. They had to stay together as a crew, even when shopping in the PX (base store), and each man stayed within sight of his roommate around the clock. The sound of a klaxon had to be obeyed instantly, even if a crewman was in the shower or fast asleep. He had to run down the ramp to his waiting "six-pack" crew truck, which would "burn rubber" to get them to their aircraft within seconds. Any crews who happened to be in the cinema at the time would see an "Alert crews respond" message appear on the screen.

The waiting time could be spent on proficiency training, college correspondence courses, or just playing card games. By the mid-1970s, alert duty was extended to a week, but family visits were allowed in a Visitation Center. Crew order briefing on weather and the latest reports on a potentially hostile situation took place at 0700hrs each day, followed by a hand-over of the eight-letter mission go-codes inside the B-52 cockpit with the bomber's previous crew. The first four letters indicated the relevant page in the code book and the rest had to match the color code and letters on the tickets kept in the double-locked "secrets box" on board the aircraft. The EW, navigator, and radar navigator all had to agree on the decoded message.

The rear gunner's position in B-52s prior to the B-52G. Tail guns were installed in all B-52s until October 1, 1991, when the gunner's position on the B-52H flight deck was removed and the tail gun system was eliminated and faired over in what was known popularly as the "Lorena Bobbitt modification." (USAF)

For an airborne alert sortie, the crew would get up at 0300hrs for an 0700hrs take-off. Lower alert levels were also maintained through unexpected "pyramid alert" phone calls in the night just to check the whereabouts of crew members. To many crews, it was like being in jail. However, Gen Power followed Gen LeMay's example in showing care for his men's welfare. He asked Congress for an extra $10 per day for alert crews due to their "real inconvenient way to live."

Dextroamphetamine "go pills" were available after briefings and crews were encouraged to take a supply with them. Aircraft commanders were handed their Combat Mission Folders, which they carried to the aircraft in a box and fastened it to a location in the cockpit, where red lighting preserved the crew's night vision. The folder contained targeting information, maps, refueling locations, and code books with other codes to arm the nuclear weapons, all secured by locks with combinations known only to the EW and radar-navigator. The target location would already be known and briefed. Robert Newton was surprised to learn that "The first target our crew was assigned was the Kremlin. What a shocker for a 2nd Lieutenant!"

The 72nd BW "crewdogs" at Ramey AFB, Puerto Rico were given three target information folders per B-52G, each containing data on six Soviet targets. The choice of targets on the day depended on a crew's distance from each potential target and its fuel status. Offset points, recognizable ground objects that gave a better radar return than the actual target, were selected and essential for the majority of potential Soviet targets. They could provide a radar fix, as some of the most vital targets, particularly missile silos, had no distinctive radar signature (no shows). Air-burst fusing was used for vulnerable above-ground targets such as airfields, while hardened targets and missile silos required the bomb to penetrate before detonation.

Targets were identified during planning, particularly those near urban areas, by using the detailed stereoscopic photographs supplied by Corona spy satellites, from the early 1960s onwards. Known threats would be marked on maps. Crews would fly to their allotted fail-safe points beyond which they would not be recalled. If they successfully attacked the first objective and managed to fly about 25 miles further, without significant damage from the first explosion, they could proceed to a second target. Exact timing and deconfliction of bombers and the effects of their weapons were obviously of great concern to crews.

Pre-flighting the B-52, taking up to three hours in peacetime, had to be accomplished within 15 minutes, so most of the checks, up to the point of starting the engines, were completed

The B-52D cockpit, with a central control area largely occupied by the eight throttles and eight sets of engine instruments. The confined B-52 crew areas were often compared to the interior space of a small car. Temperamental air conditioning, high noise levels (there was no soundproofing), and a range of industrial and other odors were all part of the crews' work conditions. (USAF)

before the aircraft was "cocked" and on alert status. "Fuel-curve" charts showing predicted fuel consumption were already prepared. Basic notes on times, callsigns, and so on, were written on windows or other suitable surfaces with Skilcraft grease pencils. The aircraft's ten hydraulic units were checked to ensure that the flying controls and undercarriage were serviceable.

For a typical practice alert take-off, the first crew member to run to the bomber opened the entry hatch and the crew clambered aboard bearing flight plans, ready meals, the coffee hot-cups, and numerous bags of documents to be stowed beside the oven. In the chilly, airless black hole the navigators set up the AN/ASQ-48 (or AN/ASQ-38 and AN/ASB-4 in the B-52E/H) bombing-navigation system to manage the mission, based on a day's preparations by the navigator. The rest of the crew would have joined him for another day of detailed planning, led by the aircraft commander and co-pilot, to establish the mission parameters including the route, likely weather, fuel load, and (crucially) exact timing based on their Emergency War Plan (EWP), or Emergency War Order, from 1960, and marked on a time-line that charted all the attacking aircraft, their routes, and times on target. As electrical power became available, the two navigators manned their equipment and received radio confirmation to take off.

A "Bravo" alert involved starting the engines, checking the go-code message and all the electronic equipment and then shutting down. A "Coco" alert was extended so that up to eight B-52s entered the runway, did a short, fast "Elephant Walk" taxi, and then returned to their alert positions for fuel replenishment and any subsequent maintenance tasks. Capt Newton recalled: "We hated Coco Alerts because it meant staying with the aircraft until they pushed it back into its spot, re-serviced it, fuelled it, and fixed any problems. We had to stay there regardless of the weather or temperature, and it normally took two hours. One time we had a blizzard and they told us the alert horn would sound only if it was 'the real thing.' You guessed it – someone didn't get the word and in the afternoon the horn blew and we raced out to our planes. You can imagine the thoughts that are going through your head when you think you are going to start a nuclear war."

Grand Forks, North Dakota, home of the 319th BW, was one of the most northerly bases. Maintainer Jim Cichocki told the author how he had to pre-flight a B-52H there at 0200hrs in conditions where the wind-chill factor caused men to work with bandages over frostbitten hands. For alert crews, every klaxon call was treated as the real thing. During one 7th BW alert exercise it sounded four times in 24 hours and each one received the correct, timed responses, although no take-offs were required.

Normal training flights could last for up to 12 hours, flying routes over the USA and often visiting several ranges en route to drop practice bombs or score radio "tones" on SAC radar sites to simulate bombing. Radio contact with these sites to arrange a drop was managed by the co-pilot. The main emphasis was on accurate navigation. Even though the potential effect of a nuclear weapon would have covered a large land area, it was still vital to pinpoint the center of a target, particularly if it was an underground missile silo. After their alert duty period, a crew had four days of "C2" time off, although they had to remain within a set distance of the base if an inspection was anticipated.

A B-52H from Minot AFB launching a Hound Dog

By 1963, SAC's *Big Four* (or Modification 1000) program equipped all B-52s, apart from early B-52Bs AGM-28 Hound Dog, ADM-20 Quail, with a new ECM suite and low-altitude interdiction upgrades. Here, we see B-52H-140-BW 60-0017 of the 450th BW at Minot AFB launching a Hound Dog at a distant enemy air defense site after the (conjectural) outbreak of hostilities with the Soviet Union a year after the Cuban Missile Crisis. Hound Dog was issued to 29 B-52 units, and it provided the first credible bomber and cruise missile combination. It was managed by the B-52 co-pilot in flight. He looked after the 42ft-long missile's J52-P-3 engine, controlling its thrust with a wafer knob throttle. Its astro-tracker computer could be used as a back-up to the B-52's. The missile's aerodynamic drag increased a B-52's fuel consumption by around 15 percent.

U.S. AIR FORCE
U.S. AIR FORCE
USAF

USAF
00017

The navigators of this early B-52B are in the pressure suits required for flights above 50,000ft as they guide the bomber using traditional distance measurement and the radar scope. (USAF)

The real thing

On northern route *Chrome Dome* patrols, a crew completed a celestial navigation section, which took it over the north polar region. A typical route from a northern base such as Westover AFB, Massachusetts, home of the 99th BW, headed out to the Atlantic over Dow, New Hampshire (passing the first of many Soviet spy trawlers), then northeast towards Goose Bay, Labrador where it reported in to *Skyking* control at SAC HQ. The message would have been noted by Soviet intelligence. The route then headed northeast to Thule, Greenland at around 36,000ft where a KC-135A waited in the Air Refueling Control Point (ARCP) area to provide enough fuel for the B-52 to reach its designated *Chrome Dome* orbit area.

On a real penetration of hostile airspace, the flight deck crew would have blanked out its cockpit vision with lead lanthanum zirconate titanite goggles and flash curtains. Any other places for the flash from a nuclear explosion to enter the aircraft's interior, such as from the optical gunsight, would also have been blanked out. Even slight light leakage could allow a flash to start a small fire in the very confined crew area if it was not fully "buttoned up." Pilots donned a piratical black eye-patch over one eye so that they would have some vision after leaving the target area with the pilot's front window partly uncurtained, or for visual bombing if the aircraft radar was knocked out by radiation. This routine had to be observed throughout the on-station section of a *Chrome Dome* flight and very soon after take-off, as the base area could have been under nuclear attack. White paint below the airframe reflected some heat and radiation. However, in nuclear tests in 1952 B-36s had large areas of white paint scorched off their lower surfaces by radiation and the blast, which also caused considerable structural damage and left one bomber so radioactive that it had to be isolated on its base for a year.

For a nuclear mission, extensive check lists were required in the hour before reaching the initial point (IP). Weapons were prepared for release and there was a scripted dialogue between the navigator, pilot, EW, and radar navigator (in many ways the most vital crew member and in practice the bombardier) to unlock, pre-arm, test, and "safety" the bombs. Full arming of the weapons was allowed 15 minutes before crossing the H-Hour Control Line, in case long-range fighters attempted to intercept the B-52s. A copper wire locking the bombs in their racks was broken by the EW pulling a D-handle. A "ready" switch was activated by the pilot after its safety wire was broken and then the radar navigator completed the arming process with a wafer switch that gave the options of "ground" or "air" burst and "safe." This was set on his DCU/9A panels (one for each bomb) after breaking another copper wire seal – a job requiring both hands and considerable effort. Each bomb contained an MC-772 ARM/SAFE switch which was then turned electrically to the red ARMED position. The computerized systems could be overridden to drop the bomb manually or abort the drop by disconnecting all the release circuits with one control.

Constant checks on the aircraft's position, heading, altitude, and speed were also needed using the MD-1 Astrocompass, N-1 magnetic compass, and APN-108 Doppler radar, updated regularly from radar and celestial observations and the radar navigator's radar tracking handle. Complex calculations ensured that the weapon was dropped from the correct point to allow for its ballistics as the aircraft began a "precision turn" towards the chosen primary and secondary IPs and then entered the bomb run. The radar navigator then put his crosshairs on the offset aiming points and instructed the pilot to center his deflection indicator. The aircraft would then be on the exact course to the target. At the appropriate point, the bomb doors would open automatically ten seconds before the drop, the aircraft would climb and the bomb would be released. If the bomber was hit en route to the target and the crew were incapacitated any pre-armed nuclear bombs, known as "special weapons," would have been released automatically, triggered by the "dead man's switch" before the aircraft crashed.

After the release of a nuclear weapon, crews had to perform a 45 to 50-degree banking turn, or "combat breakaway," to take them to their egress route. The bomber could not safely exceed 60 degrees. This regulation turn was also used during the *Linebacker II* attacks on Hanoi, Vietnam. The turn weakened the bombers' ECM protection over heavily defended targets by directing their jamming emissions away from the enemy SAM radars. For nuclear delivery, a crew with three bombs still aboard might have been required to proceed to a second target. Hardened targets such

The first external hardpoints for B-52s from the B-52C onwards were designed to carry the AGM-28 Hound Dog in the 1959 *Big Four* (Modification 1000) program. They were subsequently adapted for a wide range of weapons. In the early 1960s, the Malfunction Detection and Recording (MADREC) was installed. One of its functions was to monitor the AGM-28. Hound Dog 59-2793 is in place on B-52G-105-BW 58-0224. (Terry Panopalis collection)

EVENTS

1 Tuesday, 3 November, 1964: 1135hrs: B-52D-40-BW 56-0686 of the 86th Bomb Squadron, 494th Bomb Wing (Heavy) takes off from Sheppard AFB, Texas, and a minute later, also a second B-52D. Both carry four B28 nuclear weapons; each bomber weighs 420,000lb. They head north-east and cross the coast near Portland, Maine.

2 They pass south of Nova Scotia, then turn north to meet a KC-135A tanker at 32,000ft in the *Black Goat* air refueling area off Newfoundland. The refueling session takes 20 minutes.

3 They continue along Davis Strait into Baffin Bay, passing Thule airbase, Greenland then fly 695 miles into the Arctic Circle. Guns are briefly tested en route. Air temperature is -60F above 40,000ft and the course as straight as possible to save fuel.

4 Wednesday, 4 November: 0300hrs: They proceed towards 89 North where a full *Chrome Dome* mission would usually develop into a series of 250-mile long race-track patterns near the coast of the USSR, with each leg of the orbit taking 30 mins. This could continue for up to nine hours, patrolling about 1,300 miles of icecap.

5 They continue towards Point Barrow in Alaska and onto the Cold Coffee air refueling area to meet a tanker from Eielson AFB, Alaska. At some points the aircraft would have been in full view of Soviet radar and able to monitor radio transmissions from within northern Russia.

6 The track crosses the Aleutian Islands then reverses close to Kodiak Island. Radar contact is made with Adak Island in the Aleutians. The bombers turn south along the Canadian coast, making landfall near Portland, Oregon.

7 1120 hrs: The B-52s return to Sheppard AFB, Wichita Falls, Texas for debriefing and a 48-hour break before the next *Chrome Dome* sortie.

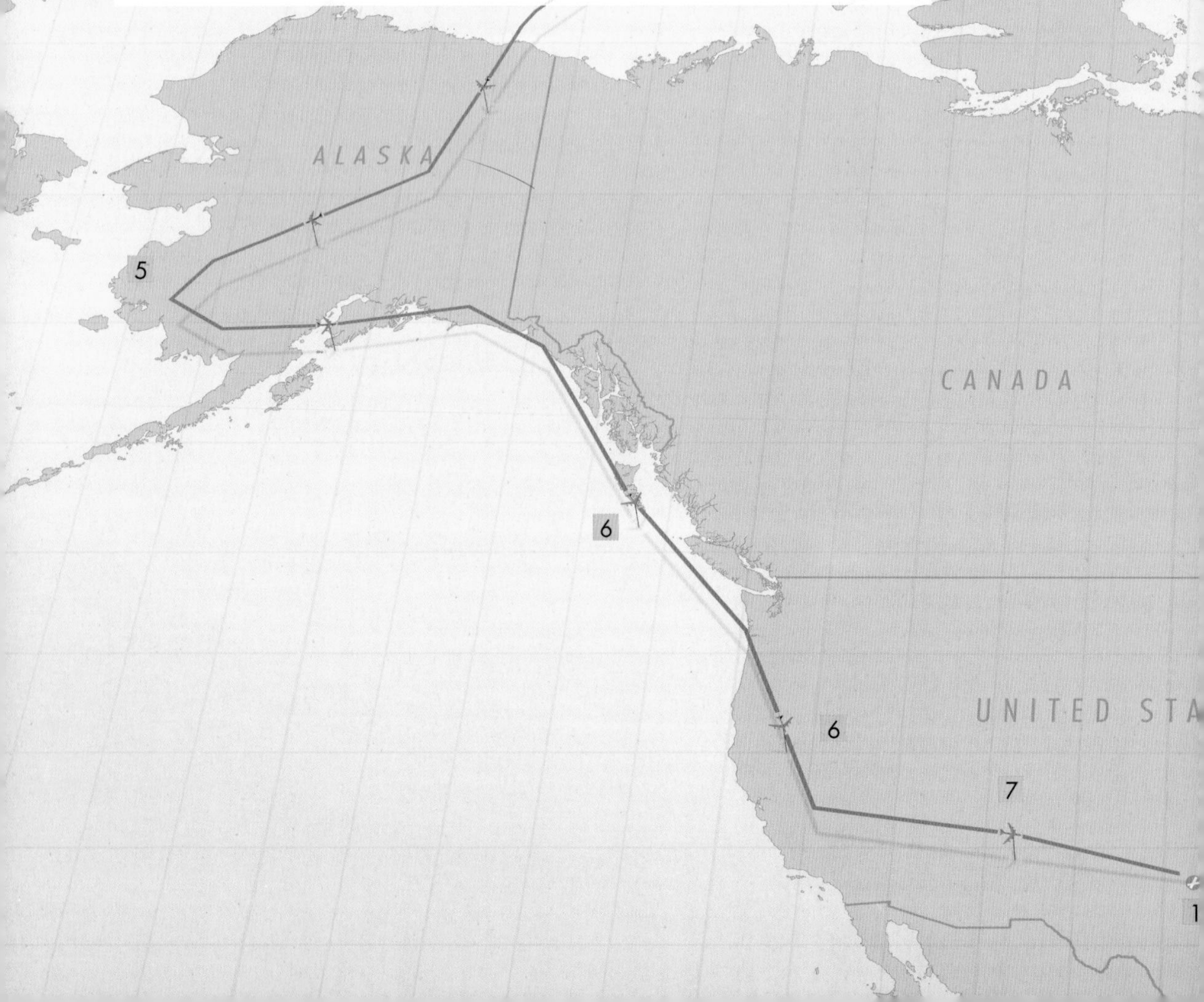

Chrome Dome northern route mission, Tuesday, November 3, 1964

Routes varied slightly during the *Chrome Dome* period. Nuclear armed B-52s were generally not allowed to cross Canadian territory but *Hard Head/Thule Monitor* routes did so.

KC-135A-05-BN refuels B-52E-90-BO 57-0014 of the 11th SW at Altus AFB, Oklahoma. As the Boeing KC-97F/G tanker's top speed was similar to the minimum speed of a B-47 or B-52, refueling had to take place at around 18,000ft in a shallow "tobogganing" dive to 12,000ft. A converted KB-47B conducted the first aerial refueling of a jet bomber by a jet tanker on September 1, 1953, but it was four years before a genuine jet tanker, the Boeing KC-135A, began deliveries to SAC. (USAF)

as underground missile silos needed several attacks. A pop-up maneuver known as "large charge" was used, in which the B-52 climbed at full power from low altitude and released one weapon, turning on a different heading to make a second attack. If it continued to survive the defenses and radiation, it then returned to low altitude on an egress course.

Returning to base was considered unlikely, as enemy missiles could well have destroyed the home airfield. Crews were given details of diversion fields, hopefully equipped with fuelling and support facilities, on the egress route, although few saw those possibilities as realistic. Even the Nevada dry lakes were considered as United States safe return areas and numerous ground alert test flights were made from several lake beds in 1962.

To the brink

During the 1962 Cuban Missile Crisis Defense Condition 3 (DEFCON-3) was enforced on October 22 for 39 hours, only the second occasion on which it had been declared, and SAC was well prepared for it. Two days later Kennedy put SAC on a higher alert condition (DEFCON-2), for the only time in history, to convince Khrushchev of the bomber force's full nuclear readiness with their potential delivery of 7,000 megatons of destruction. The rest of the forces remained at DEFCON-3. SAC leave was canceled, training interrupted, and all available bombers on 22 B-52 bases were placed on 15-minute alert and armed with nuclear weapons. The number of crews allocated to ground alert was raised to 15 per unit, so that all the available bombers were prepared. Gen Power, who had argued for airborne alert for years, was allowed to put one-eighth of his alert bombers on airborne alert, executing the previously instated *Chrome Dome* indoctrination plan. Twelve B-52 sorties were flown daily on the three *Chrome Dome/Thule Monitor* routes, beginning with the 4134th SW's B-52Fs from Mather AFB, California.

Focussing tactical air power in the southeastern USA and dispersing SAC assets required a drastic shifting of B-52s and tankers from McCoy, Homestead, and McDill AFBs to Turner and Hunter (Georgia), Sheppard (Texas) and Wurtsmith (Michigan) air bases, while Ramey AFB, Puerto Rico became a major tanker base. B-47s were dispersed to several civilian and Air National Guard airports. There were also 21 B-47s on alert at Sidi Slimane, French Morocco ready to launch against the USSR with others in the UK, while another 183 B-47s were dispersed in accordance with an existing SIOP revised plan. Those B-47s based in the eastern USA were added to the first strike bomber force, together with their KC-97 tankers. By November 1, all 84 B-58A Hustlers were ready to plug gaps in the SIOP schedule.

Col Don Blodgett flew one of those initial DEFCON-2 B-52 sorties. "After pulling up the gear and starting to climb I felt, 'This is it. I will never see my wife again.'" Maj Fred Enger also took off on a *Chrome Dome* flight at the start of the emergency. "We flew down around Detroit, to New Jersey, up the Maine coast and across to a point north of Portugal where we picked up three tankers. We then headed east out over the Mediterranean, flew over to Corsica and Sardinia, turned west to Gibraltar and up the coast of Spain, picking up another 40,000lb of fuel from two tankers. We then went north and intercepted our original track back across the Atlantic at a higher altitude, passing the eastbound pair of B-52s soon after turning west. They would not let us fly across Canada since we had four atomic bombs aboard and two Hound Dogs."

Soviet intelligence monitors were allowed to hear the B-52 crews checking in to confirm their readiness to attack. Clear text HF messages were used to ensure that Soviet listeners were well aware of SAC's determination. Battle staff were put on 24-hour alert and the number of airborne alert missions was considerably stepped up, so that 65 B-52s were following *Chrome Dome* routes at any moment, appearing on Soviet early warning radars only a few minutes apart.

Crews on the southern (Mediterranean) route were asked to look out for Soviet convoys heading into the Atlantic en route to Cuba. Soviet defenses could have calculated that a third of the 72 bombers on airborne alert were within two hours of their targets. In 1962–63 the southern route was usually flown by B-52Ds, as the B-62Hs were in a *Straight Pin* wing modification program. Airborne alert numbers remained high until November 20 when Soviet missiles and nuclear-armed Ilyushin 28 light bombers – delivered despite Khrushchev's propaganda-based assertion that "Bombers are useless. Bombers are obsolete" compared to missiles – were also finally removed from Cuba.

The crisis had prompted a rapid dispersal of SAC assets to frustrate a possible Soviet missile assault. Khrushchev would then have had to deal with far too many targets, including some whose coordinates would have been unknown to his ICBM programmers. Having fired his missiles, he would still be open to attack by considerable surviving US nuclear forces.

B-52G-125-BW 59-2577 pulls up its landing gear. The move to low-altitude penetration missions required the addition of camouflage. The SIOP color scheme was a revised version of the camouflage applied for Vietnam operations, but in a different pattern. Dark Green (FS34079), Blue Green (FS34159), and a greenish shade of Tan (FS34201) were used on B-52G/Hs from 1966 to 1967 and on some B-52E/Fs that had been equipped for Hound Dogs. It was replaced in 1984 by the Strategic Scheme using Gray (FS36081), Gunship Gray (FS36118), and Dark Green (FS34086). (USAF)

Hard Head

A parallel and equally classified *Chrome Dome*-type SAC mission from August 1961 was known as *Hard Head*, or the *Thule Monitor* Mission. Like *Chrome Dome* missions, the flights required two bombers (or occasionally a KC-135) to cruise at the best fuel conservation speed, avoiding maneuvering and unfavorable wind conditions where possible to save fuel, as there was only one scheduled tanking session per mission. *Hard Head* B-52s had to maintain constant observation at 35,000ft above the BMEWS, a radar installation at Thule, Greenland which was scanning the skies for possible Soviet missile launches. It was on the direct polar route from the Soviet Union and likely to be the USSR's first target. If a B-52 had to abort in the area, an Eielson AFB- based KC-135A had to fill in until the relief Stratofortress arrived. The monitoring nuclear-armed B-52 could report back to SAC HQ or the *Looking Glass* aircraft if contact was lost with Thule and immediately establish

B-52D-080-BO 56-0617 on approach in "Vietnam" camouflage, applied to the entire B-52D fleet from 1986 with Black (FS17038) undersides as the "antiflash" white underside finish was not required. The paint added 400lb to the overall weight. This aircraft spent most of its 24-year career on mainland US bases with brief visits to Thailand and Guam in 1973 and 1978. (USAF)

whether the loss was due to enemy action or to other causes such as a power cut. However, a nuclear attack on Thule would probably have blanked out UHF and HF communications.

Loss of contact occurred only once, on the night of November 24, 1961 in the "Black Forest Incident." A faulty microwave tower junction box near Black Forest, Colorado broke contact with Thule and Gen Power sounded the 15-minute alert, announcing that it was not a test exercise. In all, 577 armed bombers and 393 tankers prepared to roll onto their runway positions at a Coco Alert Minimum Reaction Posture to carry out the "real thing." Seconds before take-off time, the *Thule Monitor* B-52 managed to restore radio contact and the mass launch was called off. SAC's communications system clearly required improvement.

Maj Fred Enger flew *Thule Monitor* missions: "The flights were 12 hours on station plus flight time up and back. For us it was around 22 hours. We would relieve the southbound crew some 200–250 miles south of the Thule base ('little America') and bore holes for the next 12 hours apart from meeting the two tankers from Alaska." Capt Robert Newton recalled that there were occasional moments of excitement during the "twenty-two hour missions where we acted as a radio relay plane in case they could not use ground communications. We would fly a 300-mile 'bowtie' pattern over the base. The first mission flown by another outfit almost turned into a disaster. When you go that far north the true North Pole and the magnetic Pole are in opposite directions and you can't use a regular compass. You had to use a free-running gyro and polar navigation and at a certain point crank an artificial heading into it so that your directions come out right. Well, the navigator didn't do this and they went 1,100 miles off course and came close to violating Soviet airspace. One thing that inspired us to be good navigators was that if you were more than ten miles off course or five minutes out of your time limit they would scramble [USAF] fighters to identify you. If this happened, it meant an automatic $10,000 fine for you and the pilot plus the cost of sending the fighters up."

Broken Arrows

The inherent risks of flying large numbers of bombers carrying up to four nuclear weapons (one per target) on 24-hour alert led to surprisingly few mishaps among the 32 occasions since 1950 in which nuclear weapons have been lost, stolen, or destroyed in crashes, but did not cause risk of a nuclear war. No inadvertent nuclear detonations took place and there were no incidents during a three-year period of airborne alert including the peak in missions around the time of the Cuban Missile Crisis. Numerous safety devices were present in all weapons. The Department of Defense emphasized that nuclear weapons were never carried during training flights, although *Chrome Dome* missions were described as training flights. Routes were planned over sea where possible and they avoided heavily populated areas. When special weapons were being carried to foreign operational bases like Guam, B-52 crews had to check in by radio every 15 minutes.

Sixteen mishaps involving nuclear weapons in B-47, B-29, B-36, and B-50 bombers have occurred since 1950. Some weapons were never recovered, others sustained fire damage or detonation of their high explosive outer elements. The accidents involving B-52s began in October 1959. Most happened during airborne alert missions, although a few occurred during ferrying flights with weapons in transit. Although six of the nuclear devices remain undiscovered, none reached the point where a nuclear explosion could occur despite the detonation of their TNT preliminary explosives in some cases. However, they caused world-wide alarm and considerable cost. *Broken Arrow* was the code for incidents that involved potential radiation risk to the public or on a bomber base. The equivalent code for nuclear handling mishaps or security breaches on a base was *Bent Spear*. One of the earliest *Broken Arrow* incidents occurred in 1950 when a B-36 bomber crashed on an island off the coast of British Columbia due to ice and engine failure and a nuclear weapon was lost at sea.

Six *Broken Arrow* crashes involved B-52s. Most infamously, on January 17, 1966 a B-52G (58-0256) "Tea 16" of the 51st BS, 68th BW at Seymour-Johnson AFB on a *Chrome Dome* flight along the southern route collided with 910th AFRES KC-135A 61-0273 "Troubadour 14" during refueling at 31,000ft near Palomares, Spain (by agreement since 1953) and the Mediterranean. The four B28F1 weapons with Mod 3F shock-absorbing nose cones and Mod 0 parachutes were scattered. One landed near the beach, a second impacted a cemetery, and another buried itself in a tomato field. The 100ft wide retarding parachute on the fourth opened and it drifted out to sea.

Two bombs went through the preliminary high-explosive stage of detonation and nuclear debris contaminated 1,400 tons of soil and vegetation with plutonium, all of which had to be

Collision over Palomares

B-52G-115-BW 58-0256 *Tea 16* of the 51st BS, 68th BW Seymour-Johnson AFB, one of only four *Chrome Dome* airborne alert aircraft at the time on January 16/17, 1966. It took off from Seymour-Johnson AFB at dawn, reaching the furthest extent of the mission around the Soviet–Turkish border after refueling over the Golden Spur Air Refueling Area, Spain by a tanker from Torrejon *Troubadour* 11 and 13. On the return flight along the southern route it refueled over the Almeria coast from KC-135A 61-273 of the 910th ARS at Moron, piloted by Maj Emil J. Chapla. B-52G *Tea 12*, in the lead position, was being refueled by KC-135A *Troubadour 12* in the same area, the Saddle Rock Air Refueling Area. Over 750,000 SAC safe aerial refuelings had taken place since 1959, with only the October 1959 collision over Kentucky. At the height of *Chrome Dome*, refuelings were taking place every six minutes. Closing, by agreement, at a slightly higher speed than planned, *Tea 16* collided with 910th AREFS, 4130th SW, Bergstrom AFB (97th BW) KC-135A 61-0273 *Troubadour 14* during refueling at 30,500ft, two miles inland over the village of Palomares.

The accident report concluded that the staff relief pilot, World War II B-17 bomber veteran Maj Larry G. Messinger, was being given some in-flight refueling practice under the supervision of the aircraft commander, Capt Charles Wendorf. Messinger closed in on the tanker at 260kts, but then increased speed 900ft from the tanker. Advised by the KC-135A's boomer that he would "have an overrun," he activated the airbrakes before Wendorf could intervene, making the bomber pitch up and strike the tanker's underside. The 33ft long refueling probe, with a 12ft telescopic internal tube operated by MSgt Lloyd G. Potolicchio, penetrated the B-52's upper fuselage/wing joint causing an explosion and fatal damage to a longeron (spine), probably injuring the gunner and EWO and separating the left wing. Disintegration followed quickly, with the forward fuselage falling away. The fireball was seen by *Troubadour 12*'s boom operator and the tanker crew returned to see burning wreckage and the B-52's tail section and wing falling.

Fire from the B-52 explosion ignited fuel in the KC-135's refueling boom. It dived to 1,600ft where its fuel tanks with 30,000 gallons of JP-4 exploded and it hit the ground about three miles from the B-52G wreck near Palomares, a fishing village in Spain.

80256

OPPOSITE PALOMARES: AFTERMATH OF THE *BROKEN ARROW* COLLISION ON JANUARY 17, 1966

A. Major Messinger (44), the first to eject, lands 8 miles out to sea, blown offshore by high-altitude winds. He is rescued by a fishing boat.

B. Capt Ivens Buchanan ejects into a fireball and cannot separate from his seat, landing hard (the only crew member to land safely on shore) with burns and a broken shoulder.

C. Capt Wendorf (30) is injured when the forward fuselage separates from B-52G *Tea 16*. His parachute lines become tangled, but he lands safely two miles offshore and is picked up by a fishing boat.

D. Co-pilot 1Lt Richard Rooney (25), in the instructor pilot's occasional seat, bails out through the radar navigator's open hatch, fighting violent wind blasts. He is recovered by a fishing boat and later flies F-111 Aardvarks.

1Lt Stephen Montanus (navigator) is found in his seat after a failed ejection. 1Lt George Glesner (EW) and TSgt Ron Snyder (gunner) were apparently unable to eject. All four KC-135A crew perish in the crash.

The four 2,250lb B28R1 nuclear weapons, each with four parachutes, which did not open on the second bomb, fell from the wreckage as the B-52G broke up into three sections, and a huge recovery and clear-up operation ensued. Two had leaked significant quantities of plutonium radiation. Although some segments of the primary trigger of "lenses" of high explosive had detonated, they had not done so simultaneously, as required to trigger the fission primary and the thermonuclear stages. Bomb number 4 entered the sea and sank to 2,130ft, sliding down an underwater slope to a final depth of 2,550ft, five miles offshore. It was recovered by USS *Petrel* on April 7.

excavated and returned to the USA in 6,000 steel barrels for disposal. The fourth B28 landed five miles offshore in 2,500ft of water and was not located until March 15, 80 days later, by a USN submarine. The Navy's Task Force 65, commanded by RADM William Guest, used two prototype submersibles, the *Alvin* and *Aluminaut* and the USS *Petrel* to hoist the errant bomb to safety on April 7. A piece of recovery gear rented for the operation added another $50,000 a day in rental charges to the enormous $80m cost of the operation and a KC-135A had to be sent specially to take the item back to the USA.

Compensation to the Spanish government and promises to clear up the remaining soil contaminated by 25lb of plutonium in fenced-off areas continued into 2010, while disability compensation claims for US servicemen involved in the incident continued into 2021. The political furore generated by the admission that nuclear-armed SAC bombers were overflying foreign territory was a major factor in the ending of *Chrome Dome*. The southern *Chrome Dome* route was initially suspended while SAC sought to persuade Spain to allow emergency access to its airspace for armed bombers. Failure to secure agreement brought total deletion of the southern route and the overall reduction of the airborne alert force to eight B-52s

Crushed shock-absorbing nose cones identify two of the B28FI Mod Y1 nuclear weapons recovered from Palomares, Spain and displayed at the National Museum of Nuclear Science and History, Albuquerque, New Mexico. (Wiki Commons/Astor)

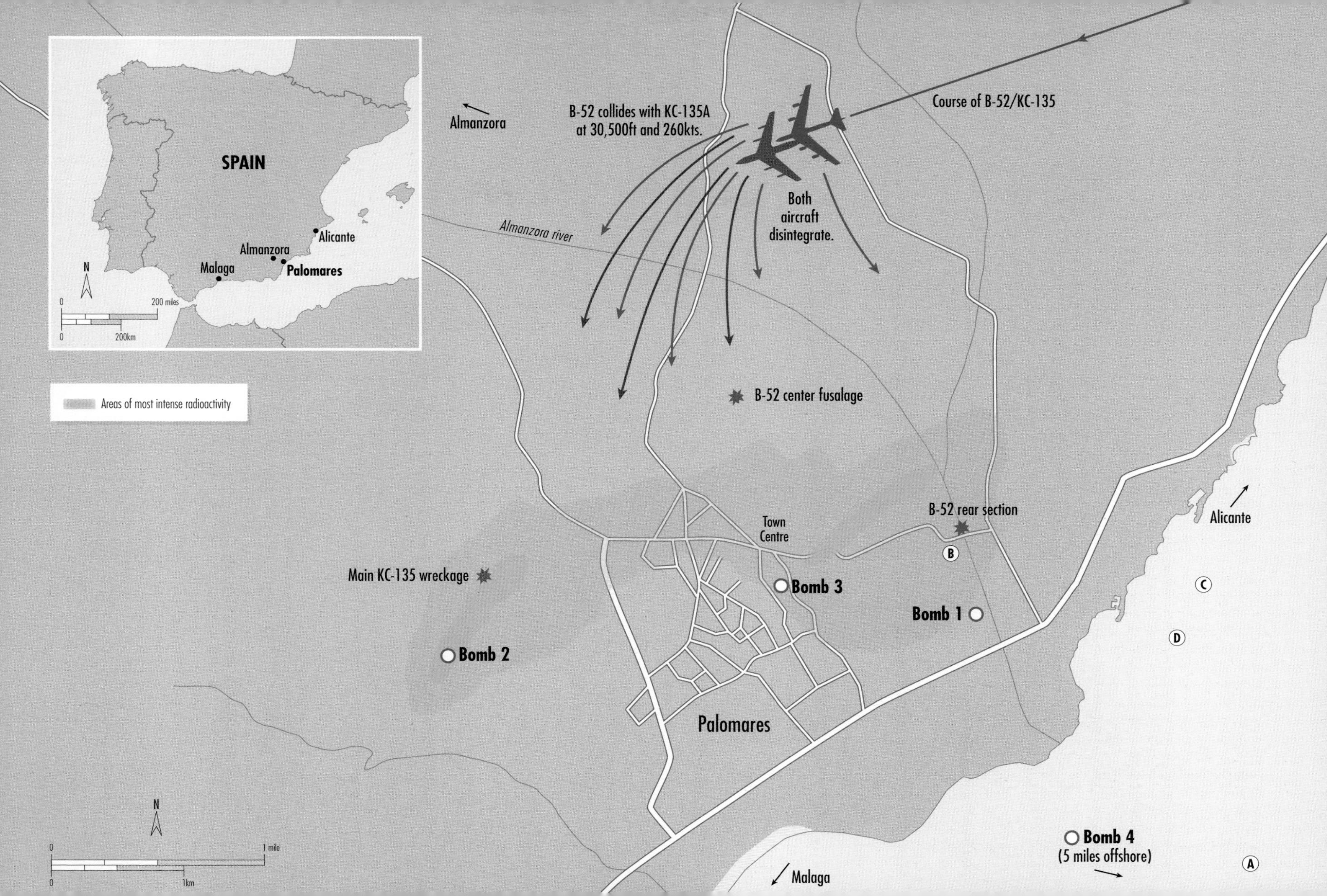

SPAIN
Alicante
Almanzora
Malaga
Palomares
N
0
200 miles
0
200km
Areas of most intense radioactivity
Almanzora
B-52 collides with KC-135A
at 30,500ft and 260kts.
Course of B-52/KC-135
Both
aircraft
disintegrate.
Almanzora river
B-52 center fusalage
Town
Centre
B-52 rear section
B
Main KC-135 wreckage
Bomb 3
Bomb 1
Bomb 2
Palomares
Alicante
C
D
Bomb 4
(5 miles offshore)
A
Malaga
N
0
1 mile
0
1km

by the end of 1966. Secretary of Defense Robert McNamara proposed the elimination of *Chrome Dome*, arguing that the improved BMEWS gave adequate time for ground alert bombers to get airborne.

He also stated that the bomber force was no longer a significant part of the US offensive capability. Airborne alert aircraft "provide us only a small capability and it has become particularly small in relation to our huge and growing missile force." Understandably, his views aroused the ire of SAC and the JCS, although Congress would have been sympathetic to his estimated saving of $123m by abolishing *Chrome Dome*. In a compromise, President Johnson agreed to four daily *Chrome Dome* missions within "the regular training program" if it "would not require additional funds." One aircraft maintained the *Thule Monitor* mission.

In modified rules, a third pilot was added for all *Chrome Dome* missions and this could be a gunner or EWO, sitting in the left seat to make sure the qualified pilot stayed awake. In any case, in 1967, SAC's Vietnam obligations reduced the total to four airborne alert sorties daily together with the *Thule Monitor* flights. Several base closures resulted, so the alert crews had to take on additional potential targets. At Sandia National Laboratories Nuclear Safety Department there were moves to improve the security of nuclear weapons, particularly the older B28 examples and replace them with a new, safer design, which became the B61.

After the official ending of *Chrome Dome*, President Nixon authorized a brief renewal in Operation *Giant Lance* from October 27, 1969. His aim was to coerce the Kremlin and Hanoi into bringing an end to the Vietnam War through a peace treaty that favored the USA. Eighteen B-52s from bases in California and Washington State were prepared for 18-hour patrols over the Alaskan *Chrome Dome* routes. However, the operation had negligible results and it was canceled three days later. (USAF)

Mainland mishaps

The first B-52 nuclear-related accident over mainland USA occurred on the night of October 14/15, 1959 when a *Steel Trap* (later, *Chrome Dome*) airborne alert B-52F 57-0036 commanded by Capt William Gutshall of the 4228th Strategic Wing (SW) at Columbus AFB, Mississippi collided with its tanker over Hardinsburg, Kentucky six minutes into a refueling session with KC-135A 57-1513 commanded by Maj Robert Imhoff. Maj Fred Enger recalled that instructor pilot Maj Milt Chatham was supervising a co-pilot, 1Lt Don Arger, who was learning to refuel in-flight when the student "got a little nervous and before Milt could do anything he pulled up into the tanker instead of pushing down. All on the tanker died." Only four B-52 crewmen, including Gutshall and Chatham, escaped the massive explosion, although the overrun speed had only been 5kts. All four of the tanker crew and four from the B-52F perished. Two unarmed "sealed-pit" nuclear weapons were recovered, one with fire damage. Enger added, "There were several changes after that. The primary crew had to be in their own seats during take-off, landing and refueling with all their gear on and parachutes hooked up."

B-52F 57-0166 sustained intolerable cabin overheating of 160°F during the first hour of a *Chrome Dome* on March 14, 1961. The 320th BW crew from Mather AFB, California felt compelled to continue the mission. They depressurized the cabin after the heat broke a windshield panel and descended below 10,000ft, heading back across the Pacific towards Mather AFB.

Their fuel consumption consequently increased and they ran out before they could meet an emergency tanker. The crew bailed out at 10,000ft leaving the captain to steer clear of populated areas and eject at 4,000ft. The aircraft crashed at Sutter Buttes near Yuba City, California. Safety devices in its tumbling W39 nuclear weapons prevented full detonation when they fell from the aircraft. Pilot error, due to the prolonged overheating and a possibility that go pills interferred with his judgment, was blamed for the failure to deal with the depressurization and fuel starvation correctly. The wing commander, Col Frank Amend, was dismissed.

A major consequence of these two potential disasters was the introduction of Permissive Action Links (PAL) at the insistence of President Kennedy. The Sandia-designed units restored full authority over the weapons to the president rather than any single military commander, except in the event of imminent war. PALs locked the weapons until a B-52 crew received an unlocking code close to their Positive Control Point.

After three years of accident-free *Chrome Domes*, structural failure caused the crew of 824th BS B-52D 55-0060 Buzz 14 to abandon their aircraft over snow-covered mountains in Maryland during a 24-hour southern route *Chrome Dome* on January 13, 1964 to a patrol area south of Turkey, with two Soviet airfields near Tbilisi as their potential target and Iran as their return destination. Their mission had been interrupted by engine trouble requiring a diversion to Moron AB, Spain. They returned to Westover AFB, Massachusetts, but a relief crew, led by Maj Thomas W. McCormick, the World War II B-29 veteran, 824th BS operations officer, flew the plane back to its Turner AFB, Georgia home. At 0130hrs over Pennsylvania, they descended and encountered severe turbulence at 29,500ft.

Climbing back to 33,000ft, Buzz 14 entered a violent storm with jet-stream winds of up to 167mph and side-force gusts of over 60mph. The vertical stabilizer and left tailplane departed, making the B-52 roll into an inverted spin, which subjected the crew to paralysing g-forces. Only four could escape, one of whom, the navigator Maj Robert Payne, slid into a freezing stream and died of his injuries, as he had not been issued winter flying gear. Gr Sgt Melvin Wooten was hit by wreckage during bail-out, breaking his leg and then freezing to death in a river. Radar navigator Maj Robert Townley went down with the aircraft, unable to strap himself back into his ejection seat fully after visiting the urinal. Maj McCormick and co-pilot Capt Parker Caswell "Mack" Peedin, who landed in a tree and fell 30ft to the ground, survived. The two 4 megaton Mk 39 Mod 1 bombs were in "tactical ferry" configuration and not connected electrically to the aircraft. Deep snow at the frozen Callahan's Swamp crash site may have helped to keep them from disintegrating, although they suffered internal damage. They were recovered by a local quarry owner who picked them up with his forklift truck and laid them on mattresses on flat-bed trucks.

A decisive *Thule Monitor/Hard Head* crash happened on January 22, 1968 when B-52G 58-0188 "Hobo 28" from the 528th BS, 380th SW at Plattsburgh, New York attempted an emergency landing at Thule AB after a cabin fire during a *Butterknife V Thule Monitor*. Third pilot Maj Alfred D'Mario had placed extra seat cushions under the navigator's seat, covering a heating vent. A heater malfunction caused bleed air from an engine to pass, uncooled, through the vent, igniting the rubber cushions. The fire extinguishers ran out and the cabin filled with smoke. Aircraft commander Capt John Haug requested an emergency landing at Thule AB, but electrical power was lost and a crash became inevitable. Six of the seven crewmen ejected at 9,000ft (the co-pilot, Leonard Svitenko, suffered fatal head injuries as he jumped out) and the bomber crashed in flames on sea ice in North Star Bay, Greenland, exploding and leaving a blackened patch covering three square miles. High explosives in the four 1.1 megaton B28FI bombs burned and there were extensive radiation leaks from 7lb of scattered plutonium.

The nine month clean-up operation, *Crested Ice*, in temperatures below –25°F, required collaboration with the Danish government, as Greenland is part of Denmark. At least two

B-52H-135-BW 60-0003 was among several B-52G/Hs used to flight test the GAM-87 Skybolt with the Air Force Flight Test Center at Edwards AFB, California in 1961 before returning to squadron service. Skybolt was a solid-fuel propelled ballistic missile for the B-52H. It delivered a W59 nuclear warhead over a 1,150-mile range, replacing Hound Dog. Spiralling costs and an inadequate airborne navigation system caused its cancelation in December 1962. (USAF)

nuclear-armed B-52s had overflown Greenland for almost ten years and there were occasional landings with tacit permission from the Danish government, which breached the country's non-nuclear policies. The story was circulated that the B-52 had been diverted to Thule rather than been on a routine flight to Thule. Some 237,000 cu ft of contaminated ice, snow and seawater had to be removed for transport to the USA and safe storage. Some of the bomb parts were believed to have fallen into the sea through ice melted by the conflagration.

The long-term consequences of this final B-52 *Broken Arrow*, and the resulting heavily publicized political tensions, were that *Hard Head* and *Chrome Dome* missions were ended on January 22, 1968. The increasing costs of airborne alert and the rapid growth of SAC's ICBM capability were also causative, but a proportion of the bomber force was kept on ground alert. Improved satellite technology was also available to give better warning of impending nuclear attack. The rules on carrying nuclear weapons over foreign terrain were revised and the telephone hotline between the US and Soviet presidents was improved to avoid false alarms.

SAC's bombers and severely overworked tanker force had to sustain its primary deterrent posture and continue to provide ground and airborne alert throughout the Vietnam War. The 320th BW at Mather AFB, California was the first to assume a dual nuclear and conventional role, although it provided a major proportion of the *Arc Light* bombing sorties over Vietnam. The number of B-52s available for SIOP inevitably decreased due to wartime duties. SAC reluctantly diverted 75 B-52s together with 53 tankers to South East Asia, beginning with a batch of 30 7th BW and 320th BW B-52Fs, which were sent to Guam late in 1965. By late 1969, over one-third of B-52s and a quarter of the tanker force were unavailable for alert duties. Crew shortages also impacted the alert posture with around 65 bombers remaining unmanned and only one crew per aircraft being available for alert rather than the usual two. America's increasing reliance on Minuteman ICBMs did much to sustain the deterrent posture during this period, including the Minuteman III with several warheads, under the control of airborne SAC command in an emergency.

ANALYSIS AND CONCLUSION

Chrome Dome missions were designed as part of a defensive shield for the free world and as an alternative to the all-out Armageddon scenario that an exchange of nuclear ICBMs or free-fall bombs would inevitably cause. The 1954 *Castle Bravo* hydrogen bomb explosion on Bikini Atoll provided a terrifying vision of the consequences. When President Kennedy, dealing with the Cuban Missile Crisis, asked his advisors how many Americans would die in a nuclear war, he was told 70 million. The airborne alert deterrent flights were also somewhat reassuring to America's allies, some of whom doubted that the nuclear trigger would be pulled on anything short of a full ICBM onslaught on the mainland USA rather than Europe. Power's outstanding achievement in generating 2,088 B-52 missions with a 97 percent in commission rate during the 30 days of the Cuban emergency, while also maintaining the SIOP schedule, was clearly a convincing justification for his highly disciplined policies.

Boredom was clearly a major aspect of 25-hour *Chrome Dome* sorties. Famously, former EW Col Marvin Howell built a 1/144th scale Revell B-52 model during a *Chrome Dome* and painted it on return to base. Model making was a favorite pastime during ground alert periods. For early B-52 training flights, the flight crew loaded their crew bus with individual briefcases full of mission details, parachutes, lunch boxes, coffee jugs, two large sextant cases, boxes of spare vacuum tubes and parts for the avionics units, and bags of clothes and personal kit in case of a diversion to another base. For alert flights, the sealed box of war mission folders was added. (USAF)

Although the United States has considered strategic bombers to be essential since World War II, there was a period following the delivery of the last B-52 in 1962 when no bombers were in production or serious development. XB-70 Valkyrie and Skybolt had been canceled and McNamara had issued a vague request for an "alternative bombing system" to follow the B-52, which he hoped to withdraw from service in the mid-1970s "if necessary." This was effectively a life extension, as the bomber was originally meant to have begun retirement in 1964. McNamara still prioritized long-range missiles in 1964, but he sought to reassure SAC that the experience of supersonic flight gained from XB-70 and FB-111A testing would be useful in studies for an advanced manned strategic aircraft (AMSA). It would be a "long-range, low altitude penetrator to serve as an airborne missile launcher" within SIOP.

The collapse of the Soviet Union in the early 1990s meant that SIOP could be substantially scaled down. This seismic change was marked by the visit of two 2nd Wing B-52Gs to Dyagilevo, Russia in March 1992 and a reciprocal visit to Barksdale AFB by two Tu-95 *Bear* bombers and their An-124 *Condor* tanker. A few months previously, both bases would have been targets.

With the Soviet threat substantially reduced, US bomber and tanker fleets were cut back, with most KC-135As going into storage. SAC's alert forces were stood down on September 27, 1991. Base closures were quickly implemented and in June 1992 SAC itself gave way to a unified Strategic Command to manage all US nuclear capable assets including submarines and radar alert facilities. The Alert Force, suspended during *Desert Storm*, was subjected to a progressive drawdown from September 28, 1991. Although Strategic Air Command's days ended in the June 1992 USAF reorganization, the B-52's importance was recognized by the new Air Combat Command for delivery of conventional weapons, or by Strategic Command (which managed all nuclear bomber, submarine, or strategic missiles) if its nuclear capability was called upon. In both capacities, the strong SAC link with the JCS, which Curtis LeMay had fostered, was ended.

In 1988, TSgt Timothy P. Carroll of the 2nd BW was interviewed about his job, and he observed: "This job takes a lot of dedication, especially for a plane as old as the B-52. Everyone knows that there are very few B-52 pilots older than the aircraft they are flying. There's probably not a crew chief as old as a B-52." He could be forgiven for not realizing that his comments were made roughly one-third of the way through the bomber's career and just before one of its most notable wartime performances in Operation *Desert Storm*.

There is little doubt that SAC's airborne alert force served its purpose, although many would argue that in retrospect it was, in its early days, a sledgehammer to crack a nut. However, in the words of the early 1950s' Secretary of the Air Force, Donald A. Quarles, "Atomic weapons and the capability of the United States to deliver them have represented the major deterrent to aggressive inclinations of the Communist Bloc." Winston Churchill shared that view: "The Strategic Air Command is a deterrent of the highest order in maintaining ceaseless readiness. We owe much to their devotion to the cause of freedom in a troubled world." Col Phil Rowe's assessment of airborne alert missions was a little more practical. "They were horrendously expensive, wore out planes and equipment and really only protected one-fourth of the bomber fleet. It was limited nuclear deterrence at best."

Costs were indeed staggering. When 12 B-52s were flying *Chrome Domes*, their annual fuel and spares bill was $65m. Each sortie used $7,000 of fuel. Gen Power's request to increase the airborne alert force to 25 percent of SAC's strength would have added $750m to the $8bn allocated to SAC.

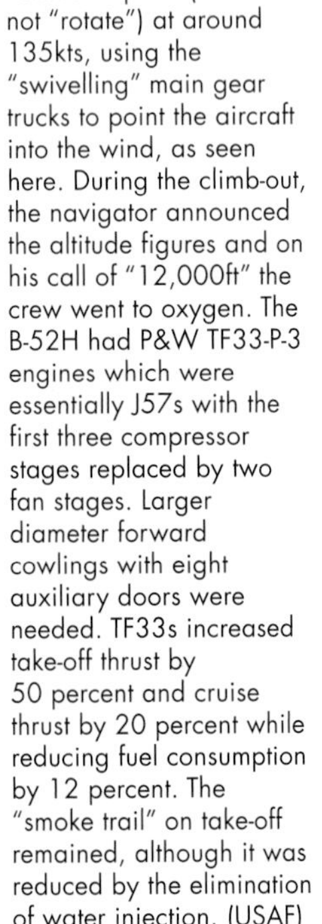

Early B-52s reached "unstick" speed (B-52s do not "rotate") at around 135kts, using the "swivelling" main gear trucks to point the aircraft into the wind, as seen here. During the climb-out, the navigator announced the altitude figures and on his call of "12,000ft" the crew went to oxygen. The B-52H had P&W TF33-P-3 engines which were essentially J57s with the first three compressor stages replaced by two fan stages. Larger diameter forward cowlings with eight auxiliary doors were needed. TF33s increased take-off thrust by 50 percent and cruise thrust by 20 percent while reducing fuel consumption by 12 percent. The "smoke trail" on take-off remained, although it was reduced by the elimination of water injection. (USAF)

The Cold War involved very little shooting, but several intelligence-gathering aircraft were shot down and over 2,600 SAC combat crew were lost in various mishaps as they performed their arduous duties in very stressful conditions. Generally, their efforts went unrecognized by higher authority. Medals were awarded for B-52 *Arc Light* sorties over South Vietnam, but not for *Chrome Domes*. Generations of B-47 and B-52 crews struggled to maintain SAC's deterrent from bases like Grand Forks, North Dakota where 8ft of snow could cover the base and bombers had to take off in temperatures of –30°F. If they had failed, the situation would have been catastrophically different. The macabre mathematics of nuclear war used human casualty statistics as the measure of relative success in battle. In 1964, the US National Security Council anticipated 93 million American deaths from a Soviet first strike, with 140 million Soviet casualties from an American response. Only 20 percent of that first strike would have involved Soviet missiles. Continued no-win exchanges would have increased that number to 700 million, on both sides. At the least, there was always the possibility that *Broken Arrow* situations or launching the hair-trigger alert forces in response to a false alarm or human error on either side of the Iron Curtain could have led quickly to an irretrievable situation. NORAD computer errors caused hundreds of bombers to move to advanced alert stages in the 1980s, including one incident in which a radar interpreted the rising moon as an incoming barrage of Soviet ICBMs. Over 60 *Broken Arrow* incidents probably occurred, subject to future declassification of documents.

Over 60 years since the Cuban Missile Crisis, that potentially apocalyptic situation still remains. As Gen "Hap" Arnold observed after the first nuclear attack ended the war with Japan, "The influence of atomic energy on air power can be stated very simply. It has made air power all-important." Ironically, that importance, expressed in the doctrine of Mutually Assured Destruction (MAD), was a vital factor in securing the longest period of peace between the world's major powers since the Treaty of Westphalia ended the Thirty Years' War in Europe in 1648. For many veterans, there is no doubt that it was SAC that won the Cold War.

BIBLIOGRAPHY

Adams, Chris, *Inside the Cold War* (Air University Press, Maxwell AFB, 1999)

Borgiasz, William S., *The Strategic Air Command* (Praeger Publishers, 1996)

Boyne, Walter J., *Boeing B-52: A Documentary History* (Schiffer Publishing Ltd, 1994)

Brewer, Alex P., Jr, *A Navigator's Odyssey* (Amazon, 2018)

Coremans, Danny, *Uncovering the Boeing B-52H* (Daco Publications, 2008)

Darling, Kev, *Boeing B-52A-F Stratofortress* (Guideline Publications, 2021)

Davies, Peter E., *B-52 Stratofortress vs SA-2 Guideline SAM* (Osprey Publishing, 2018)

Davies, Peter E., Thornborough, T. and Cassanova, T., *Boeing B-52 Stratofortress* (Crowood Aviation Series, 1998)

Deaile, Melvin G., *Always at War, Organizational Culture in Strategic Air Command 1946–62* (Naval Institute Press, 2018)

Dobbs, Michael, *One Minute to Midnight* (Arrow Books, 2009)

Dobson, Joel, *The Goldsboro Broken* Arrow (Lulu, 2013)

Dorr, Robert F. and Peacock, Lindsay, *B-52 Stratofortress* (Osprey Aerospace, 1995)

Francillon, René J. and Lewis, Peter B., *B-52, Ageing BUFFS, Youthful Crews* (Osprey Publishing, 1988)

Habermehl, C. Mike and Hopkins, Robert S., *Boeing B-47 Stratojet* (Crécy Publishing Ltd, 2018)

Harder, Robert O., *Flying from the Black Hole* (Naval Institute Press, 2009)

Harten, Don, *Collision Over Vietnam* (Turner Publishing Co., 2011)

Hastings, Max, *Abyss – The Cuban Missile Crisis 1962* (William Collins, 2022)

Hopkins, Robert S., *Boeing KC-135 Stratotanker* (Midland Publishing Ltd, 1997)

Jenkins, Dennis R. and Rogers, Brian, *Boeing B-52G/H Stratofortress* (Aerofax, Inc., 1990)

Kozak, Warren, *LeMay, the Life and Wars of General Curtis LeMay* (Regnery History, 2009)

Lake, Jon, *B-52 Stratofortress Units in Combat 1955–73* (Osprey Publishing, 2004)

Lloyd, Alwyn T., A *Cold War Legacy* (Pictorial Histories Publishing Co., 1999)

McGill, Earl J., *Jet Age Man* (Helion and Company, UK, 2012)

Newhouse, John, *War and Peace in the Nuclear Age* (Vintage Books, New York, 1990)

Peacock, Lindsay, *Boeing B-47 Stratojet* (Osprey Publishing, 1987)

Stein, Allan T., *Into the Wild Blue Yonder – My Life in the Air Force* (Texas A&M University Press, 2005)

Yenne, Bill, B-*52 Stratofortress* (Zenith Press, 2012)

Zeybel, Henry, *Along for the Ride, Navigating Through the Cold War, Vietnam, Laos and More* (Casemate Publishers, 2021)

Ziarnick, Brent D., *To Rule the Skies – General Thomas S. Power and the Rise of Strategic Air Command in the Cold War* (Naval Institute Press, 2021)

Documents

Building a Strategic Air Force (W.S. Moody, Air Force History and Museums Program, 1995)

Burr, William (ed.), *Crises, Alerts and DEFCONs, 1961–76 Part 2* (The Nuclear Vault, 2021)

Grant, Rebecca, "The Perils of Chrome Dome" (*Air Force Magazine*, August 2011)

History of the Custody and Deployment of Nuclear Weapons, July 1945 through September 1977 (Office of the Assistant to the Secretary of Defense, Atomic Energy, 1978)

Hopkins III, Robert S., *How the Strategic Air Command Would Go to Nuclear War* (National Security Archive, 2019)

Kaplan, Edward, *To Kill Nations* (Cornell University, Ithaca, undated)

Narrative Summaries of Accidents Involving US Nuclear Weapons, 1950–1980 (Department of Defense, 1981)

Robinson, Bill, "A Hard Day's Night" (*Smithsonian Magazine*, Sept 2006)

Seventy Years of Strategic Air Refueling, 1918–1988 (Office of the Historian, HQ SAC, Offutt AFB, May 1990)

SIOP Targeting Philosophy (Office of the Secretary of Defense, April 1977)

Strategic Air Command Operations in the Cuban Missile Crisis of 1962 (SAC HQ Historical Study No. 90, Vol.1, declassified 1992)

Strategic Air Warfare, an Interview with Generals Curtis LeMay, Leon W. Johnson, David A. Burchinal and Jack J. Catton (Office of Air History "Project Warrior", Washington, DC, 1988)

The Strategic Air Command Alert System 1956–70 (SAC History Study 129, HQ SAC, 1973)

T.O. 1B-52C-1 B-52C/D Flight Manual, June 1967 (Secretary of the Air Force)

T.O. 1B-52E-1 B-52E/F Flight Manual, November 1962 (Secretary of the Air Force)

T.O. 1B-52G-1 B-52G Flight Manual, June 1975 (Secretary of the Air Force)

T.O. 1B-52H-1 B-52H Flight Manual, August 1996 (Secretary of the Air Force)

AN 01-20ENA-1 B-47 Flight Handbook, July 1950 (Secretary of the Air Force)

INDEX